Ann B. Gill
What is the sunship of beleu

P9-DGT-913

ROMANS

Chapters 9—16

J. Vernon McGee

THOMAS NELSON PUBLISHERS

Nashville • Atlanta • London • Vancouver

Published in Nashville, Tennessee, by Thomas Nelson, Inc.

Scripture quotations are from the KING JAMES VERSION of the Bible.

Library of Congress Cataloging-in-Publication Data

McGee, J. Vernon (John Vernon), 1904–1988
   [Thru the Bible with J. Vernon McGee]
   Thru the Bible commentary series / J. Vernon McGee.
      p.   cm.
   Reprint. Originally published: Thru the Bible with J. Vernon
McGee. 1975.
   Includes bibliographical references.
   ISBN 0-7852-1047-4 (TR)
   ISBN 0-7852-1106-3 (NRM)
   1. Bible—Commentaries. I. Title.
BS491.2.M37 1991
220.7′7—dc20   90–41340
                                          CIP

Printed in the United States of America

2 3 4 5 6 7 8 9 — 99 98 97 96 95

CONTENTS

ROMANS—Chapters 9—16

PREFACE

The radio broadcasts of the Thru the Bible Radio five-year program were transcribed, edited, and published first in single-volume paperbacks to accommodate the radio audience.

There has been a minimal amount of further editing for this publication. Therefore, these messages are not the word-for-word recording of the taped messages which went out over the air. The changes were necessary to accommodate a reading audience rather than a listening audience.

These are popular messages, prepared originally for a radio audience. They should not be considered a commentary on the entire Bible in any sense of that term. These messages are devoid of any attempt to present a theological or technical commentary on the Bible. Behind these messages is a great deal of research and study in order to interpret the Bible from a popular rather than from a scholarly (and too-often boring) viewpoint.

We have definitely and deliberately attempted "to put the cookies on the bottom shelf so that the kiddies could get them."

The fact that these messages have been translated into many languages for radio broadcasting and have been received with enthusiasm reveals the need for a simple teaching of the whole Bible for the masses of the world.

I am indebted to many people and to many sources for bringing this volume into existence. I should express my especial thanks to my secretary, Gertrude Cutler, who supervised the editorial work; to Dr. Elliott R. Cole, my associate, who handled all the detailed work with the publishers; and finally, to my wife Ruth for tenaciously encouraging me from the beginning to put my notes and messages into printed form.

Solomon wrote, ". . . of making many books there is no end; and much study is a weariness of the flesh" (Eccl. 12:12). On a sea of books that flood the marketplace, we launch this series of THRU THE BIBLE with the hope that it might draw many to the one Book, *The Bible.*

J. Vernon McGee

The Epistle to the
ROMANS

INTRODUCTION

Let me say just a word concerning Paul the apostle. With his writings we actually come now to a different method of revelation. God has used many ways to communicate to man. He gave the Pentateuch—the Law—through Moses. He gave history, He gave poetry, and He gave prophecy. He gave the Gospels, and now we come to a new section: the Epistles, the majority of which were written by Paul.

Adolf Deissmann tried to make a distinction between epistles and letters. Having examined the papyri that were found at Oxyrhynchus in Egypt, he made a decision between literary and nonliterary documents, placing the epistles of Paul in the latter category, thereby making them letters rather than epistles. However, a great many scholars today think this is an entirely false division.

These letters that we have—these epistles—are so warm and so personal that, as far as you and I are concerned, it is just as if they came by special delivery mail to us today. The Lord is speaking to us personally in each one of these very wonderful letters that Paul and the other apostles wrote to the churches. Nevertheless, Romans contains the great gospel manifesto for the world. To Paul the gospel was the great ecumenical movement and Rome was the center of that world for which Christ died. Paul's Epistle to the Romans is both an epistle and a letter.

Paul made this statement in Romans 15:15–16, "Nevertheless, brethren, I have written the more boldly unto you in some sort, as putting you in mind, because of the grace that is given to me of God, that I should be the minister of Jesus Christ to the Gentiles, ministering the gospel of God, that the offering up of the Gentiles might be acceptable, being sanctified by the Holy Ghost." Paul made it very clear here that he was the apostle to the Gentiles. He also made it clear that Simon Peter was the apostle to the nation Israel. For instance, in Galatians he said, "(For he that wrought effectually in Peter to the apostleship of the circumcision, the same was mighty in me toward the Gentiles:) And when James, Cephas, and John, who seemed to be pillars, perceived the grace that was given unto me, they gave to me and Barnabas the right hands of fellowship; that we should go unto the heathen, and they unto the circumcision" (Gal. 2:8–9). Therefore you see that Paul was peculiarly the apostle to the Gentiles. When you read the last chapter of Romans and see all those people that Paul knew, you will find that most of them were Gentiles. The church in Rome was largely a gentile church.

Paul also made the point that, if somebody else had founded the church in Rome, he would never have gone there. Instead, he said that he was eager to go there. "So as much as in me is, I am ready to preach the gospel to you that are at Rome also" (Rom. 1:15). He wanted to go to Rome to preach the gospel. In Acts 26 Paul recounted to Agrippa the message the Lord gave to him when He appeared to him: "Delivering thee from the people, and from the Gentiles, unto whom now I send thee, to open their eyes, and turn them from darkness to light, and from the power of Satan unto God, that they may receive forgiveness of sins, and inheritance among them which are sanctified by faith that is in me" (Acts 26:17–18).

Further, Paul would never have gone to Rome, although he was eager to go, if anyone else had preached the gospel there ahead of him. In Romans 15:20 he said, "Yea, so have I strived to preach the gospel, not where Christ was named, lest I should build upon another man's foundation." Paul, my friend, just didn't go where another apostle had been. We can conclude, therefore, that no other apostle had been to Rome.

Now that leads me to say a word about Rome, and the question is: Who founded the church in Rome? I am going to make a rather unusual statement here: Paul is the one who founded the church in

Rome, and he founded it, as it were, by "long distance" and used the "remote control" of an apostle to write and guide its course.

Let me make this very clear. You see, Rome was a tremendous city. Paul had never been there, no other apostle had been there, and yet a church came into existence. How did it come into existence? Well, Paul, as he moved throughout the Roman Empire, won men and women to Christ. Rome had a strong drawing power, and many people were in Rome who had met Paul throughout the Roman Empire. You might ask, "Do you know that?" Oh, yes, we have a very striking example of that in Acts where we find Paul going to Corinth. "After these things Paul departed from Athens, and came to Corinth; and found a certain Jew named Aquila, born in Pontus, lately come from Italy, with his wife Priscilla; (because that Claudius had commanded all Jews to depart from Rome:) and came unto them. And because he was of the same craft, he abode with them, and wrought: for by their occupation they were tentmakers" (Acts 18:1–3). Paul had met Aquila and Priscilla—their home was in Rome, but there had been a wave of anti-Semitism; Claudius the emperor had persecuted them, and this couple had left Rome. They went to Corinth. We find later that they went with Paul to Ephesus and became real witnesses for Christ. Then, when Paul wrote the Epistle to the Romans, they had returned to Rome, and Paul sent greetings to them. We do have this very personal word in Acts concerning this couple. What about the others? Well, Paul did know them. That means he had also met them somewhere and had led them to Christ. Paul was the founder of the church at Rome by "long distance"—by leading folk to Christ who later gravitated to Rome.

Paul knew Rome although he had not been inside her city limits at the time of the writing of the Roman epistle. Rome was like a great ship passing in the night, casting up waves that broke on distant shores. Her influence was like a radio broadcast, penetrating every corner and crevice of the empire. Paul had visited Roman colonies such as Philippi and Thessalonica, and there he had seen Roman customs, laws, languages, styles, and culture on exhibit. He had walked on Roman roads, had met Roman soldiers on the highways and in the marketplaces, and he had slept in Roman jails. Paul had appeared before Roman magistrates, and he had enjoyed the benefits of Roman citizenship. You see, Paul knew all about Rome although he was yet to visit there. From the vantage point of the world's capital, he was to preach the global gospel to a lost world that God loved so much that He gave His Son to die, that whosoever believed on Him might not perish but have eternal life.

Rome was like a great magnet: It drew men and women from the ends of the then-known world to its center. As Paul and the other apostles crisscrossed in the hinterland of this colossal empire, they brought multitudes to the foot of the Cross. Churches were established in most of the great cities of this empire. In the course of time, many Christians were drawn to the center of this great juggernaut. The saying that "all roads lead to Rome" was more than just a bromide. As Christians congregated in this great metropolis, a visible church came into existence. Probably no individual man established the church in Rome. Converts of Paul and the other apostles from the fringe of the empire went to Rome, and a local church was established by them. Certainly, Peter did not establish the church or have anything to do with it, as his sermon on Pentecost and following sermons were directed to Israelites only. Not until the conversion of Cornelius was Peter convinced that Gentiles were included in the body of believers.

Summarizing, we have found that Paul is the one writing to the Romans. He was to visit Rome later, although he knew it very well already. And Paul was the founder of the church in Rome.

As we approach this great epistle, I feel totally inadequate because of its great theme, which is the righteousness of God. It is a message that I have attempted over the years to proclaim. And it is the message, by the way, that the world today as a whole does not want to hear, nor does it want to accept it. The world likes to hear, friend, about the glory of mankind. It likes to have mankind rather than God exalted. Now I am convinced in my own mind that any ministry today that attempts to teach the glory of man—which does not present the total depravity of the human family and does not reveal that man is totally corrupt and is a ruined creature, any teaching that does not deal with this great truth—will not lift mankind, nor will it offer a remedy. The only remedy for man's sin is the perfect remedy that we have in Christ, that which God has provided for a lost race. This is the great message of Romans.

Friend, may I say to you that the thief on the cross had been declared unfit to live in the Roman Empire and was being executed. But the Lord Jesus said that He was going to make him fit for heaven and told him, ". . . Today shalt thou be with me in paradise" (Luke 23:43). God takes lost sinners—like I am, like you are—and He brings them into the family of God and makes them sons of God. And He does it because of Christ's death upon the Cross—not because there is any merit in us whatsoever. This is the great message of Romans.

It was Godet, the Swiss commentator, who said that the Reformation was certainly the work of the Epistle to the Romans (and that of Galatians also) and that it is probable that every great spiritual renovation in the church will always be linked both in cause and in effect to a deeper knowledge of this book. It was Martin Luther who wrote that the Epistle to the Romans is "the true masterpiece of the New Testament and the very purest Gospel, which is well worthy and deserving that a Christian man should not only learn it by heart, word for word, but also that he should daily deal with it as the daily bread of men's souls. It can never be too much or too well read or studied; and the more it is handled, the more precious it becomes, and the better it tastes."

Chrysostom, one of the early church fathers, had the epistle read to him twice a week. And it was Coleridge who said that the Epistle to the Romans was the most profound writing that exists. Further, we find that one of the great scientists turned to this book, and he found that it gave a real faith. This man, Michael Faraday, was asked on his deathbed by a reporter, "What are your speculations now?" Faraday said, "I have no speculations. My faith is firmly fixed in Christ my Savior who died for me, and who has made a way for me to go to heaven."

May I say to you, this is the epistle that transformed that Bedford tinker by the name of John Bunyan. A few years ago I walked through the cemetery where he is buried, and I thought of what that man had done and said. You know, he was no intellectual giant, nor was he a poet, but he wrote a book that has been exceeded in sales by only one other, the Bible. That book is Bunyan's *Pilgrim's Progress*. It is a story of a sinner saved by grace, and that sinner was John Bunyan. And the record of history is that this man read and studied the Epistle to the Romans, and he told its profound story in his own life's story, the story of Pilgrim—that he came to the Cross, that the burden of sin rolled off, and that he began that journey to the Celestial City.

Let me urge you to do something that will pay you amazing dividends: read the Book of Romans, and read it regularly. This epistle requires all the mental make-up we have, and in addition, it must be bathed in prayer and supplication so that the Holy Spirit can teach us. Yet every Christian should make an effort to know Romans, for this book will ground the believer in the faith.

OUTLINE

I. **Doctrinal, Chapters 1—8**
("Faith")
A. Justification of the Sinner, Chapters 1:1—5:11
    1. Introduction, Chapter 1:1–17
        (a) Paul's Personal Greeting, Chapter 1:1–7
        (b) Paul's Personal Purpose, Chapter 1:8–13
        (c) Paul's Three "I Am's," Chapter 1:14–17
           (Key verses, 16–17—the revelation of the righteousness of God)
    2. Revelation of the Sin of Man, Chapters 1:18—3:20
      (This is "Sinnerama." Universal fact: Man is a sinner. Ecumenical movement is away from God. Axiom: World is guilty before God—all need righteousness.)
        (a) Revelation of the Wrath of God Against Sin of Man, Chapter 1:18–32
           (1) Natural Revelation of God (Original Version), Chapter 1:18–20
           (2) Subnatural Response of Man (Revision), Chapter 1:21–23
           (3) Unnatural Retrogression of Man (Perversion), Chapter 1:24–27
           (4) Supernatural Requittal of God (Inversion), Chapter 1:28–32
        (b) Revelation of the Sin of Good People, Chapter 2:1–16
           (Respectable people need righteousness.)
        (c) Revelation of the Sin of Israel Under Law, Chapters 2:17—3:8
        (d) Revelation of the Universality of Sin, Chapter 3:9–20
           (1) Judge's Verdict of Guilty Against Mankind, Chapter 3:9–12
           (Man cannot remove guilt.)

Sonship— is both male and female —
@ offspring of Abraham

election —

CHAPTER 9

Taken for Israel

THEME: *Israel defined; Israel identified; the choice of
Israel is in the sovereign purpose of God; the choice
of Gentiles in the scriptural prophecies*

We now have come to the second major division of this epistle.
Romans chapters 1—8 is *doctrinal*. Romans chapters 9—11 is
dispensational. Romans chapters 12—16 is *duty*. The first eight chapters of Romans emphasize *faith*. Chapters 9—11 emphasize *hope*.
Chapters 12—16 emphasize *love*. There is another way to view Romans: The first section deals with *salvation*; the second section with
segregation; and the last section with *service*.

Paul has concluded the first eight chapters of Romans, and he has
put salvation on a broad basis, because the entire human race is lost.
"For all have sinned, and come short of the glory of God" (Rom. 3:23).
God has made salvation available to everyone on one basis alone—
faith in the Lord Jesus Christ. Paul is now ready to discuss the second
major division.

Some have attempted to dismiss this section by labeling it an ap-
pendix. Others minimize its importance by terming it a parenthesis
and not actually pertinent. However, it is not only pertinent, it is vital
to the logic and doctrine of the epistle.

There is a sense in which chapters 8 and 12 can be joined together
as two boxcars. But Paul was not making up a freight train when he
wrote Romans. Romans is not a freight train but a flowing stream.
Chapters 9—11 can no more be removed than you can take out the
middle section of the Mississippi River without causing havoc. Griffith Thomas writes, "The chapters 9-10-11 are an integral part of the
epistle and are essential to its true interpretation."

There are certain grand particulars which reveal the significance
of this section. They are: The psychological factor; the historical factor; the doctrinal factor.

The *psychological factor* has to do with the personal experience of the apostle Paul. It is not entirely accurate to state that Romans comes from the head of the apostle and Galatians comes from his heart. The heart of Paul is laid bare in the opening of chapter 9—and in fact, throughout this section. There is a great gap between chapter 8 and chapter 9. Chapter 8 closes on the high plane of triumph and joy in the prospect of no separation from the love of God in Christ Jesus our Lord. Chapter 9 opens on the low plane of despair and sorrow. Obviously a change of subject matter brought about this heartbreak in the apostle. This we shall observe when we consider the text.

The *historical factor* takes into account the unique position and problem in Paul's day. Modern interpretation has largely failed to take into consideration this factor. The present-day church is for the most part Gentile, and the Jewish background has been all but forgotten. Men assume that the Old Testament promises are merged and dissolved into the church. The arbitrary assumption is that the church is heir to the prophecies of the Old Testament and that God is through with the nation Israel.

Some time ago a Christian organization held a prophetic congress in Jerusalem. It was rather amusing because a meeting that was to be so important ended up as a "tempest in a teapot." Many writers who covered the congress said that the city of Jerusalem did not even know that it was taking place. It is interesting to compare this congress with the Council at Jerusalem in Acts 15 when the whole city was shaken. Half of those present in the congress had no place for the nation Israel in God's plan for the future. They felt that God was through with Israel. If that were true, why did they go to Jerusalem to hold a prophetic congress? They could have gone just as well to Scappoose, Oregon, or Muleshoe, Texas. God is not by any means through with Israel, as we shall see. Stifler states this view:

It has been tacitly assumed in Christian interpretation that Judaism's day is over; that an elect, leveling church built on faith in Christ was the intent of the law and the prophets; and that it was the duty of all Jews to drop their peculiarities and come into the church. Such an assumption the Jews ascribed to Paul. It is strangely forgotten that the mother church in Jerusalem and Judaea never had a Gentile within its fold, that none could have been admitted, and that every member of that primitive body of tens of thousands was zealous of the law (Acts 21:20). They accepted Jesus as the Messiah, but abandoned none of their Old Testament customs and hopes. Christianity has suffered not a little in the continuous attempt to interpret it not from the Jewish, but from the Gentile point of view. The church in Jerusalem, and not the church in Antioch or Ephesus or Rome, furnishes the only sufficient historic outlook (James M. Stifler, *The Epistle to the Romans*, p. 162).

My friend, it is a very narrow view to assume that God is through with the nation Israel. Paul's answer to, "Hath God cast away his people?" is a sharp negative: "God forbid" (Rom. 11:1). He is going to show that the promises that God made to the nation Israel are going to be fulfilled to that nation. Also he will show that God has made certain promises to the church, and today He is calling out an elect people, both Jew and Gentile, to form the church. This is exactly the conclusion to which the Council at Jerusalem came (Acts 15). This is actually the crux of the interpretation of prophecy: "And after they had held their peace, James answered, saying, Men and brethren, hearken unto me: Simeon hath declared how God at the first did visit the Gentiles, to take out of them a people for his name. And to this agree the words of the prophets; as it is written, After this I will return, and will build again the tabernacle of David, which is fallen down; and I will build again the ruins thereof, and I will set it up: That the residue of men might seek after the Lord, and all the Gentiles, upon whom my name is called, saith the Lord, who doeth all these things. Known unto God are his works from the beginning of the world" (Acts 15:13–18).

James is making it very plain that God is calling out a people to His name. When He concludes this, He will remove the church from the earth and will turn again to Israel. But even at that time, God is not through with Gentiles. We are told that all the saved Gentiles at that time will enter the Kingdom with Israel, and God's Kingdom will be set up on this earth. This historical factor cannot be ignored.

The doctrinal factor concerns the right dispensational interpretation and the sovereign purposes of God. Paul has traced in the first eight chapters the great subjects of sin, salvation, and sanctification— all the way from grace to glory. In this age, nationality, ritual, and ceremonies have no weight before God. Faith is the only item which God accepts from man. Any person, regardless of race or condition, can find mercy. This does seem to level out the very distinctions made in the Old Testament. But Paul is going to answer that, and he begins by the rhetorical question: "Hath God cast away his people?" (Rom. 11:1). The answer, of course, is that He has not. Paul began this epistle, you remember, by saying that the gospel is "to the Jew first" (Rom. 1:16), which I think means that chronologically it was given to the Jew first.

Chapters 9—11 is a very important section. It may not deal with Christian doctrine, but it deals with the eschatological, that is, the prophetic, section of the Bible that reveals God is not through with Israel.

Now as we begin chapter 9, notice that this has to do with God's past dealings with Israel. In chapter 10 we will see God's present dealings with Israel and, in chapter 11, God's future dealings with Israel as a nation. God's reason for dealing with the nation in the past did not derive from their exceptional qualities or superior efforts. On the contrary, all of God's actions are found in His own sovereign will. He functions through mercy in His dealings with Israel and all others— with you and me. Luther's statement affords a fitting introduction to this chapter. "Who hath not known passion, cross, and travail of death cannot treat of foreknowledge (election of grace) without injury and inward enmity toward God. Wherefore take heed that thou drink not wine while thou art yet a sucking babe." This is strong medicine we are going to look at here.

ISRAEL DEFINED

I say the truth in Christ, I lie not, my conscience also bearing me witness in the Holy Ghost [Rom. 9:1].

Paul said he was the chief of the sinners

Let me give you my translation of this verse: I speak the truth in Christ, I do not lie, my conscience in the Holy Spirit bearing witness with me.

This seems to be a very formal introduction coming from the apostle Paul, but you must remember that at the time he wrote this he was accused of being an enemy of his own people. We are told in Acts 23:12, "And when it was day, certain of the Jews banded together, and bound themselves under a curse, saying that they would neither eat nor drink till they had killed Paul." Now Paul uses an expression that is a favorite with him: "I tell the truth, I do not lie."

> **that I have great heaviness and continual sorrow in my heart [Rom. 9:2].**

It is impossible for us to appreciate adequately the anguish of this great apostle for his own nation. His patience in the presence of their persistent persecution is an indication of it. He knew how they felt toward Christ and toward Christianity, for he once felt that way himself. He had been a Pharisee, a leader; he longed for them to come to Christ as he had.

> **For I could wish that myself were accursed from Christ for my brethren, my kinsmen according to the flesh [Rom. 9:3].**

I'd like to give you a different translation of this: For I was wishing (but it is not possible) that I myself were accursed (devoted to destruction) from the Christ for the sake of my brethren, my kinsmen according to the flesh.

The verse presents a real problem in translation. If you want a free translation, here it is: For I was once myself accursed from Christ as my brethren, my kinsman according to the flesh.

Frankly, I do not understand Paul at all, if our Authorized Version has translated it accurately. Paul has just said in chapter 8 that nothing

move from tradition to

can separate us from the love of God, which is in Christ Jesus. Now Paul says, "I wish I were accursed." That is idle wishing, Paul. You can't be accursed—you just told us that. This, then, is just an oratorical gesture; you are not sincere when you say a thing like this.

However, the apostle Paul is always sincere. He didn't use oratorical gestures. So I believe he is saying, "For I was once myself accursed from Christ just like my brethren. I know I cannot be accursed, and I want them to come to know Christ and be in my present position." Professor J. A. Bengel said, "It is not easy to estimate the measure of love in a Moses and a Paul." Moses expressed the same sentiment in Exodus 32:31–32, "And Moses returned unto the LORD, and said, Oh, this people have sinned a great sin, and have made them gods of gold. Yet now, if thou wilt forgive their sin—; and if not, blot me, I pray thee, out of thy book which thou hast written."

> **Who are Israelites; to whom pertaineth the adoption, and the glory, and the covenants, and the giving of the law, and the service of God, and the promises;**
>
> **Whose are the fathers, and of whom as concerning the flesh Christ came, who is over all, God blessed for ever. Amen [Rom. 9:4–5].**

Paul raises the question: Who are Israelites? There are eight things that identify Israelites:

1. *The Adoption.* The adoption was national and pertained to the national entity, not to separate individuals. The only nation that God ever called His "son" is the nation Israel: "And thou shalt say unto Pharaoh, Thus saith the LORD, Israel is my son, even my firstborn" (Exod. 4:22). Again in Deuteronomy 7:6, "For thou art an holy people unto the LORD thy God: the LORD thy God hath chosen thee to be a special people unto himself, above all people that are upon the face of the earth." Either God meant this or He did not mean it. And if He didn't mean it, then I don't know why you believe in John 3:16—both promises are in the same Book. I believe John 3:16, and I believe Deuteronomy 7:6. He said "When Israel was a child, then I loved him, and

called my son out of Egypt" (Hos. 11:1). God speaks of the nation—not just an individual—the *nation* of Israel as being His son. He never said that of any other people. The *adoption* belongs to Israel.

2. *The Glory*. This was the physical presence of God with them as manifested in the tabernacle and later in the temple. Exodus 40:35 reveals, "And Moses was not able to enter into the tent of the congregation, because the cloud abode thereon, and the glory of the LORD filled the tabernacle." The children of Israel are the only people who have ever had the visible presence of God. There is no visible presence of God today. We need to remember that fact.

Many years ago there was an evangelist who put up a tent in Southern California. He bragged that you could see angels walking on top of the tent and that you could see angels inside the tent. The minute he made a statement like that I knew there was something radically wrong. I also knew there was an explanation, and there was—the man died an alcoholic. I imagine that, after two or three drinks, you could see angels walking on tents, and he probably did. But only Israel truly had the visible presence of God. The church does not have it. Why? Because the Spirit of God indwells every believer, making real the living Christ who is at God's right hand.

3. *The Covenants*. God has made certain covenants with the nation Israel that He intends to carry out. Many of them He has already carried out. He said He would make them a blessing to all people. He said to David that this One would come in his line. All of this has been fulfilled in the Lord Jesus Christ. God made many covenants with Israel—with Abraham, with David, with the nation—which He has not made with any other people. To Israel belong the covenants.

4. *The Law*. The Mosaic Law was given to the nation Israel. "Now therefore, if ye will obey my voice indeed, and keep my covenant, then ye shall be a peculiar treasure unto me above all people: for all the earth is mine" (Exod. 19:5). Then God says in Exodus 31:13, "Speak thou also unto the children of Israel, saying, Verily my sabbaths ye shall keep: for it is a sign between me and you throughout your generations; that ye may know that I am the LORD that doth sanctify you." This is for the nation Israel, you see.

I have been asked, "Why don't you keep the Sabbath Day?" I do not keep it because I am not a member of the nation Israel. Others have asked me, "Did God ever change the Sabbath Day?" God has not changed the Sabbath, but He has sure changed us. We are in Christ, and that is a new relationship. He gave the Mosaic Law to Israel.

5. *The Service of God*. This had to do with the worship of the tabernacle and temple. They were to be a kingdom of priests. "And ye shall be unto me a kingdom of priests, and an holy nation. These are the words which thou shalt speak unto the children of Israel" (Exod. 19:6). The nation failed God, but God did not give up His purpose that they should be priests. God took the tribe of Levi and gave them the responsibility of serving and caring for the tabernacle and, later on, the temple. In the future, in the millennial Kingdom the nation Israel will once again be God's priests upon the earth. *Isaiah 9:6 7*

6. *The Promises*. The Old Testament abounds with promises made to these people. God told Joshua, "Moses my servant is dead; now therefore arise, go over this Jordan, thou, and all this people, unto the land which I do give to them, even to the children of Israel" (Josh. 1:2). The children of Israel were to possess the land. I was over there some time ago, but I didn't cross the Jordan because it wasn't safe—probably someone would have shot at me. Several years ago I did cross the Jordan River, but not because God gave a command to Joshua and the people of Israel. I have never felt that any of the land of Palestine belonged to me. The land is beginning to bloom like a rose, but much of that land is still barren. It will be a beautiful land again when the Lord Jesus comes to rule. It has never been my land, and it never will be. The land of Palestine was given strictly to the Jews.

7. *The Fathers*. This refers primarily to Abraham, Isaac, and Jacob.

8. *Christ the Messiah*. He came according to the flesh. When He came to this earth, He was a Jew. The woman at the well called Him a Jew (see John 4:9). Paul is careful to say that we know Him no longer after the flesh: "Wherefore henceforth know we no man after the flesh: yea, though we have known Christ after the flesh, yet now henceforth know we him no more" (2 Cor. 5:16). Paul identifies Jesus as God, and to Paul He is the God-Man. John 1:14 tells us, "And the Word was made flesh, and dwelt among us, (and we beheld his glory, the glory as of the only begotten of the Father,) full of grace and truth." Christ

9. provide a line to christ
matthew 1:1-16

came as a human babe to the nation Israel. The woman at the well identified Him as a Jew, and I think she was in a better position to say who He was than some scholar in New York City sitting in a swivel chair in a musty library.

Perhaps "Christ the Messiah" should be separated from the other seven features because it is greater than all the others. "For verily he took not on him the nature of angels; but he took on him the seed of Abraham" (Heb. 2:16).

ISRAEL IDENTIFIED

The Israel of another time period has already been defined. Now let us identify them in Paul's day and in our day also.

Not as though the word of God hath taken none effect. For they are not all Israel, which are of Israel [Rom. 9:6].

This is a strange expression. In other words, not all the offspring, the natural offspring of Israel, are the real Israel. The Jew in Paul's day raised the question as to why the Jew had not wholeheartedly accepted Christ since theirs was an elect nation. Is not this failure on God's part? Paul partially dealt with this problem at the beginning of Romans 3. Now Paul is going to make a distinction between the natural offspring of Jacob and the spiritual offspring. Always there has been a remnant, and that remnant, whether natural or not natural, has been a spiritual offspring. This is a distinction within the nation Israel, and he is not including Gentiles here at all. The failure was not God's; but the people had failed. God's promises were unconditional.

Neither, because they are the seed of Abraham, are they all children: but, In Isaac shall thy seed be called [Rom. 9:7].

This verse is a devastating blow to the argument of those who were attempting to stand against Paul. If the "seed" were reckoned on natural birth alone, then the Ishmaelites, Midianites, and Edomites would be included. A fine Arab man in Jericho said to me several years ago, "I want you to know that I am a son of Abraham." I could not argue against that. He *was* a son of Abraham. These others were all the physical offspring of Abraham. To be the natural offspring of Abraham was no assurance that a person was a child of promise.

You will recall what the Jews said to the Lord Jesus on one occasion, ". . . Abraham is our father. Jesus said unto them, If ye were Abraham's children, ye would do the works of Abraham." Then the Lord continued saying, "Ye are of your father the devil, and the lusts of your father ye will do. He was a murderer from the beginning, and abode not in the truth, because there is no truth in him. When he speaketh a lie, he speaketh of his own: for he is a liar, and the father of it" (John 8:39, 44).

> **That is, They which are the children of the flesh, these are not the children of God: but the children of the promise are counted for the seed [Rom. 9:8].**

The apostle Paul makes a clear distinction between the elect and the nonelect in the nation Israel. "The children of the flesh" are not the children of God. "The children of the *promise*" are the ones counted for the seed. In Acts 21:20 Dr. Luke tells us, "And when they heard it, they glorified the Lord, and said unto him, Thou seest, brother, how many thousands of Jews there are which believe; and they are all zealous of the law." There were in Israel *thousands* of Jews who turned to Christ after His death and resurrection. They were the *elect*, and Paul always called them "Israel." When we come to the Book of the Revelation where our Lord was speaking to the churches (the turn of the first century), He says to them in effect, "They do not even belong to a synagogue that worships Me any longer; it is a synagogue that worships Satan" (see Rev. 2:9; 3:9).

> **For this is the word of promise, At this time will I come, and Sarah shall have a son [Rom. 9:9].**

The children of the promise are not those who believed something—
Isaac did not *believe* before he was born! Isaac was the promised seed.
God promised, and God made good.

Now we are coming to some strong statements.

**And not only this; but when Rebecca also had conceived
by one, even by our father Isaac [Rom. 9:10].**

Isaac and Rebecca are likewise given as an illustration of this principle of the divine election. *Why were the Children not
the elect of God*

**(For the children being not yet born, neither having done
any good or evil, that the purpose of God according to
election might stand, not of works, but of him that call-
eth;) [Rom. 9:11].**

Although this verse is in parentheses, its truth is of supreme importance. Some explanation may be offered for God's rejection of Ish-
mael, but that is not possible in the case of Isaac and Rebecca's
children—those boys were twins! God rejected the line of primogeni-
ture, that is, of the first born, and chose the younger son. At that time
Jacob had done no good, and Esau had done no evil. It does not rest
upon birth—that was identical—and it does not rest upon their character or their works. Paul makes the entire choice rest upon "the *purpose* of *God* according to election." He further qualifies his statement
that it is not of works, but rests upon God who calls. However, the
calling in this verse is not to salvation.

**It was said unto her, The elder shall serve the younger
[Rom. 9:12].**

This is a quotation from Genesis 25:23, which was given before the
two boys were born. "And the LORD said unto her, Two nations are in
thy womb, and two manner of people shall be separated from thy
bowels; and the one people shall be stronger than the other people;
and the elder shall serve the younger." *How many
Find the offspring of Ismel & Genesis
Isaac
& Esau
13:25*

As it is written, Jacob have I loved, but Esau have I hated [Rom. 9:13].

This is a quotation from the last book in the Old Testament (see Mal. 1:2–3). This statement was not made until the two boys had lived their lives and two nations had come from them, which was about two thousand years later, and much history had been made. A student once said to Dr. Griffith Thomas that he was having trouble with this passage because he could not understand why God hated Esau. Dr. Thomas answered, "I am having a problem with that passage too, but mine is different. I do not understand why God *loved* Jacob." That is the big problem. It is easy to see why God rejected Esau, friend. He was a rascal; he was a godless fellow, filled with pride, and from him came a nation that wanted to live without God and turned their backs upon Him. I can understand why God rejected Esau, but not why He chose Jacob. The Bible tells us that He made His choice according to His sovereign will.

THE CHOICE OF ISRAEL IS IN THE SOVEREIGN PURPOSE OF GOD

What shall we say then? Is there unrighteousness with God? God forbid [Rom. 9:14].

What will we say to this? Is there injustice with God? Perish the thought! Let is not be. The answer is a resounding *no*!

The natural man rebels against the sovereignty of God. If anything is left to God to make the choice, man immediately concludes that there is injustice. Why is that?

There are people today who have applauded some of the presidents we have had during the 1960s and 1970s. Apparently—I don't know if we will ever get the truth—there have been bad judgments made during their terms in office, and as a result thousands of our boys have died. Yet one of those men received more votes than any man who has run for president. The remarkable thing is that we often do not question the judgments of men, but we do question the judgments of God.

My friend, although we cannot intrude into the mysterious dealings of God, we can trust Him to act in justice. We cannot avoid the
doctrine of election, nor can we reconcile God's sovereign election
with man's free will. Both are true. Let's keep in mind that this is His
universe. He is sovereign. I am but a little creature on earth, and He
could take away the breath from me in the next moment. Do I have the
audacity to stand on my two feet, look Him in the face, and question
what He does? That would be rebellion of the worst sort. I bow to my
Creator and my Redeemer, knowing that whatever choice He makes is
right. By the way, if you do not like what He does, perhaps you should
move out of His universe and start one of your own so you can make
your own rules. But as long as you live in God's universe, you will
have to play according to His rules. Little man needs to bow his stiff
neck and stubborn knees before Almighty God and say, "There is no
unrighteousness with Thee" (see John 7:18).

> **For he saith to Moses, I will have mercy on whom I will
> have mercy, and I will have compassion on whom I will
> have compassion [Rom. 9:15].**

Moses, you recall, wanted to see the glory of God. God said in effect,
"I'll show it to you, Moses, but I'll not show it to you because you are
Moses." Now, Moses was a very important person. He was leading the
children of Israel through the wilderness. God says, "I will have compassion on whom I will have compassion. I will do this for you, not
because you are Moses, but because I am God!" Do you know why
God saved me? It was not because I am Vernon McGee, but because He
is God. He made the choice, and I bow before Him.

> **So then it is not of him that willeth, nor of him that run-
> neth, but of God that sheweth mercy [Rom. 9:16].**

God's mercy is not extended as a recognition of human will, nor is it a
reward of human work. Human-willing and human-working are not
motivating causes of God's actions. Man thinks that his decision and
his effort cause God to look with favor upon him. Stifler states it suc-

cinctly when he says, "Willing and running may indicate the posses-
sion of grace, but they are not the originating cause" (*The Epistle to
the Romans*, p. 172). God extends mercy, and He does it because he is
God, my friend. Who are we to question Him? I bow before Him today.

> **For the scripture saith unto Pharaoh, Even for this same
> purpose have I raised thee up, that I might shew my
> power in thee, and that my name might be declared
> throughout all the earth.**

> **Therefore hath he mercy on whom he will have mercy,
> and whom he will he hardeneth [Rom. 9:17–18].**

God says that He used Pharaoh. "But," you may say, "he was not
elected." No, he sure wasn't. Just think of the opportunities God gave
him. Pharaoh would have said, "I am Pharaoh. I make the decisions
around here. I reject the request to let the people of Israel go." God
says, "You may think you won't, but you are going to let them go."
God's will prevails. When the Scriptures say that God hardened Pharaoh's heart, it means that God forced Pharaoh to make the decision
that was in his heart. God forced him to do the thing he wanted to do.
There never will be a person in hell who did not choose to be there,
my friend. You are the one who makes your own decision.

> **Thou wilt say then unto me, Why doth he yet find fault?
> For who hath resisted his will? [Rom. 9:19].**

This is the reasoning of the natural man: If God hardened the heart of
Pharaoh, why should he find fault with Pharaoh? Wasn't he accomplishing God's purpose?

> **Nay but, O man, who art thou that repliest against God?
> Shall the thing formed say to him that formed it, Why
> hast thou made me thus? [Rom. 9:20].**

Human reasoning is not the answer to the problem. The answer is found only in the mystery and majesty of God's sovereignty. Faith leaves it there and accepts it in humble obedience. Unbelief rebels against it and continues on under the very wrath and judgment of the God it questions.

John Peter Lange has well stated it: "When man goes the length of making himself a god whom he affects to bind by his own rights, God then puts on His majesty, and appears in all His reality as a free God, before whom man is nothing, like the clay in the hand of the potter. Such was Paul's attitude when acting as God's advocate in his suit with Jewish Pharisaism. This is the reason why he expresses only *one* side of the truth."

> You cannot put one little star in motion;
> You cannot shape one single forest leaf,
> Nor fling a mountain up, nor sink an ocean,
> Presumptuous pigmy, large with unbelief!
>
> You cannot bring one down of regal splendor,
> Nor bid the day to shadowy twilight fall,
> Nor send the pale moon forth with radiance tender;
> And dare you doubt the One who has done it all?
> —Sherman A. Nagel, Sr.

The important thing is that God is *God*, and little man won't change that.

In the next few verses Paul uses the illustration of the potter and the clay. God is the Potter and we are clay. God took man out of the dust of the earth and formed him. He didn't start with a monkey—man made a monkey of himself, but God didn't make him like that. God took man from the dust of the ground. The psalmist says, ". . . he remembereth that we are dust" (Ps. 103:14). We forget this sometimes. As some wag has said, when dust gets stuck on itself, it is mud. Abraham took his correct position before God when he said, ". . .

Behold now, I have taken upon me to speak unto the Lord, which am but dust and ashes" (Gen. 18:27).

> **Hath not the potter power over the clay, of the same lump to make one vessel unto honour, and another unto dishonour? [Rom. 9:21].**

God reaches into the same lump of humanity and takes out some clay to form Moses. Again, He reaches in and takes out of the same lump the clay to make Pharaoh. It was all ugly, unlovely, sightless, and sinful clay at the beginning. His mercy makes a vessel "unto honour"; that is, a vessel for honorable use. It is the Potter's right to make another vessel for "dishonour" or common use.

> **What if God, willing to shew his wrath, and to make his power known, endured with much longsuffering the vessels of wrath fitted to destruction.**
>
> **And that he might make known the riches of his glory on the vessels of mercy, which he had afore prepared unto glory,**
>
> **Even us, whom he hath called, not of the Jews only, but also of the Gentiles? [Rom. 9:22–24].**

Paul has already established the fact that God is free to act in the mystery and majesty of His sovereignty. Now Paul shows that God deals in patience and mercy even with the vessels of wrath. God did not fit them for destruction; the rebellion and sin of the clay made them ripe for judgment. God would have been right in exercising immediate judgment, but He dealt with these vessels, not as lifeless clay, but as creatures with a free will. He gave them ample opportunity to reveal any inclination they might have of obeying God. Although God hates sin and must judge it in a most final manner, His mercy is constantly going out to the creatures involved.

God suggests that the "vessels of wrath" are the Jewish nation, which was destroyed in A.D. 70. Jesus, you recall, announced this destruction, but He wept over the city, and he prayed, ". . . Father, forgive them . . ." (Luke 23:34). When the final judgment came in A.D. 70, God saved a remnant. These were "vessels of mercy."

THE CHOICE OF GENTILES IN THE SCRIPTURAL PROPHECIES

This is the final division of the chapter. Paul has made it very clear that the nation Israel was chosen by the sovereign will of God, not because of their merit. God not only chose a nation and not only saved those in that nation who turned to Him—and it's a remnant always— but among the Gentiles He is calling out a people today to His name.

> **As he saith also in Osee, I will call them my people, which were not my people; and her beloved, which was not beloved.**

> **And it shall come to pass, that in the place where it was said unto them, Ye are not my people; there shall they be called the children of the living God [Rom. 9:25–26].**

"Osee" is the Greek name of the prophet Hosea. This is a quotation from Hosea 2:23, and it refers to the nation Israel. Peter refers this prophecy to the believing remnant in his day which perpetuated the nation. To his people who had turned to Christ, he says, "But ye are a chosen generation, a royal priesthood, an holy nation, a peculiar people; that ye should shew forth the praises of him who hath called you out of darkness into his marvellous light: which in time past were not a people, but are now the people of God: which had not obtained mercy, but now have obtained mercy" (1 Pet. 2:9–10).

The second prophecy (v. 26) is from Hosea 1:10 and refers to Gentiles anyplace on the earth who turn to Christ now and in the future. As James put it: "That the residue of men might seek after the Lord, and all the Gentiles, upon whom my name is called, saith the Lord, who doeth all these things" (Acts 15:17).

And so God reached into Europe. He did not send the gospel into

Europe because the people there were superior. Some members of the
white race seem to think that they are superior people. They are not.
The Chinese were way ahead of my ancestors in Paul's day. My
ancestors—and perhaps yours—were there in the forests of Europe. A
branch of my family was over in Scotland. I am told they were the
dirtiest, filthiest savages who have ever been on this earth. Do you
think God carried the gospel to them because they were superior?
They were anything but that. "It is not of him that willeth, nor of him
that runneth, but of God that sheweth mercy" (v. 16). I thank Him for
that—how wonderful it is!

> **Esaias also crieth concerning Israel, Though the number of the children of Israel be as the sand of the sea, a remnant shall be saved:**

> **For he will finish the work, and cut it short in righteousness: because a short work will the Lord make upon the earth [Rom. 9:27–28].**

A literal translation would be: Isaiah also cried in anguish over Israel,
if the number of the sons of Israel be as the sand of the sea, the remnant only shall be saved; for He [the Lord] will execute His word upon
the earth, finishing and cutting it short in righteousness.

The quotation Paul uses is from Isaiah 10:22–23. Only a remnant
of Israel will be saved in the Great Tribulation period. If you want to
see the percentage, there are approximately fifteen million Jews today.
In the Great Tribulation period we know that only 144,000 Jews will
be sealed—that is a small ratio. While I do believe others will be saved
during that period, 144,000 will be His witnesses, and a small remnant will be saved. It has always been only a remnant with them, and
it is only a remnant with Gentiles. Now don't ask me why—it is God
that shows mercy. If He saved only *one*, it would reveal the mercy of
God, because none of us deserve His mercy.

> **And as Esaias said before, Except the Lord of Sabaoth had left us a seed, we had been as Sodoma, and been made like unto Gomorrha [Rom. 9:29].**

In this verse Paul is quoting from Isaiah 1:9. This is a startling statement, but it is a fitting climax to the sovereignty of God. Even the elect nation would have been like Sodom and Gomorrah in depravity and rebellion to God if He had not intervened in sovereign mercy and recovered a remnant. What an indictment of proud Pharisaism and proud church membership today! Only God's mercy keeps any of us from going to hell, my beloved.

> **What shall we say then? That the Gentiles, which followed not after righteousness, have attained to righteousness, even the righteousness which is of faith [Rom. 9:30].**

This is a thrilling statement. Gentiles, without willing or working, found righteousness in Christ because *God* worked and *God* willed it. The Old Testament Scriptures had prophesied it. As we have seen, Isaiah had said that Gentiles were to be saved.

> **But Israel, which followed after the law of righteousness, hath not attained to the law of righteousness [Rom. 9:31].**

In other words, Israel, pursuing after a law which should give righteousness, did not arrive at such a law. This is a terrifying statement. The Jews tried to produce a righteousness of their own through the Mosaic system. They didn't produce it—look at the nation today. Religious people are the most difficult people to reach with the gospel—church members, who think they are good enough to be saved.

You will never be able to reconcile the sovereignty of God and the responsibility of man. But Paul is making it very clear here that if you are going to be saved it is your responsibility. It is "whosoever will may come" (see Mark 8:34) and ". . . him that cometh to me I will in no wise cast out" (John 6:37). You can come; don't stand on the sidelines and say, "I'm not elected." But I have never heard of anybody being elected who didn't run for office. If you *want* to be saved, you are the elect. If you don't, you're not. And that is all I know about it. I cannot reconcile election and free will. I have come to the place in the sunset of my life that I can say that God is sovereign, and He is going to do this according to His will. And His will is right—there is no unrighteousness with Him. He won't make a mistake. Men make mistakes; men in government make mistakes, yet people believe in them. My friend, why don't you believe in God? He is righteous, He is good, and whatever He does is right.

> **Wherefore? Because they sought it not by faith, but as it were by the works of the law. For they stumbled at that stumblingstone;**

> **As it is written, Behold, I lay in Sion a stumblingstone and rock of offence: and whosoever believeth on him shall not be ashamed [Rom. 9:32–33].**

The quotation here is from both Isaiah 8:14 and Isaiah 28:16. The Jews stumbled. To the Gentile the Cross is foolishness. The one who believes, either Jew or Gentile, will be saved. The humble mind will come in simple faith. The natural man will still try to produce salvation by some natural process. He will try to reconcile the sovereignty of God and the responsibility of man as if the puny mind of man is capable and infallible.

CHAPTER 10

THEME: *Present state of Israel; present standing of Israel; present salvation for both Jew and Gentile*

We have seen the present state of Israel; they are lost. And that is their condition today. They are lost just as the Gentiles are lost. The reason is that Christ is the end of the law of righteousness.

Now Paul turns from the sovereignty of God to the responsibility of man. He began this thought in the concluding verses of chapter 9.

PRESENT STATE OF ISRAEL

Brethren, my heart's desire and prayer to God for Israel is, that they might be saved [Rom. 10:1].

They are responsible, you see; they are responsible to God. Our Lord has said to them, "For the days shall come upon thee, that thine enemies shall cast a trench about thee, and compass thee round, and keep thee in on every side. And shall lay thee even with the ground, and thy children within thee; and they shall not leave in thee one stone upon another; because thou knewest not the time of thy visitation" (Luke 19:43–44). That is the condition of the nation over there today. They are surrounded by nations that want to push them into the sea. Why? You can blame the Arab, you can blame Russia, you can blame everybody. You can blame God if you want to, because He says the reason they are in such a state—unable to have peace—is that they did not recognize their time of visitation. So Paul says, "My heart's desire and prayer to God for Israel is, that they might be saved." Now notice the three great features in His statement:

1. Israel, with all it possessed (see Rom. 9:4–5) of religion, was not saved. May I say that probably 75 percent of church members are not saved. They are just members of a religious club. They are in rebellion against God in that they will not accept the righteousness God

offers in Christ. You can be religious and *lost*. Israel had a God-given religion, but they needed to be saved. They had religion but not righteousness. They had more than any other nation, but they were lost. Paul's desire was that Israel might be saved.

2. Israel was savable. Bengel says, "Paul would not have prayed had they been altogether reprobate." They were savable. Who would have thought that my ancestors in the forests of Germany were savable? They were as heathen as anyone could possibly be. Yet at that time the Chinese had a civilization. Why didn't the missionaries go in that direction? Why didn't the apostles say, "Let's not bother with those pagan Gentiles; they are not even savable"? Pagan Gentiles were savable, and the Jews were savable also.

3. They are on the same plane before God today as Gentiles and should be evangelized as any other people without Christ. There is no difference today. "For all have sinned, and come short of the glory of God" (Rom. 3:23). The idea of a superior race or an inferior race is ridiculous. The ground at the foot of the Cross is all level. Whoever you are, your social position, your church membership, your good works, or the color of your skin will not help you. Without Christ you are a hell-doomed sinner. God is just and righteous when He says that to you. Perhaps you say, "I don't like what that preacher said," Well, it is actually what God said, my friend. God is putting it in neon lights here. He doesn't want you to miss it.

There are those today who believe that the gospel ought to go to Israel first. I think Paul meant that chronologically it went to the Jew first. For the first few years in the city of Jerusalem and in all Israel there was not a Gentile saved. The church was 100 percent Jewish. Although I do not believe we are told to evangelize the Jew first in our day, I certainly do believe that the Jew should not be left out. He is in the plan and purpose of God, and he should have the gospel. I disagree with a man like the late Dr. Reinhold Niebuhr, a recent liberal theologian, who is reported to have said (by *Time* magazine in 1958), "Do not try to convert Jews . . . Jews may find God more readily in their own faith than in Christianity." He maintains this viewpoint, so he says, "especially because of the guilt they are likely to feel if they become Christians." However, coming to Christ is the way to get rid of guilt. They should have the gospel—all people should have it. God is prepared to show mercy today.   *devotion*

For I bear them record that they have a zeal of God, but not according to knowledge [Rom. 10:2].

I know some churches, friend, where the members are as busy as termites. On Monday night they play basketball. On Tuesday night it is football. On Wednesday night it is volleyball. On Thursday night it is baseball. On Friday night they just "have a ball." They have something going on every night. They have a "zeal of God"—they like to do it all in the name of Jesus. But all they have is religion. My friend, do you have Christ? Have you accepted the righteousness that God offers in Christ Jesus? You cannot be saved on any other basis. You have to be *perfect* to go to heaven, and I have news for you: you are not perfect. Neither am I perfect. But I am going to heaven because Jesus died for me, was buried, and rose again from the dead. He was delivered for my offenses and was raised for my justification. He is my righteousness. I will go to heaven one day because He took my place. Is Jesus Christ your Savior? Forget your church membership for awhile. I do not mean to minimize your membership, but do not trust it for salvation. The average church today is as dead as a dodo bird. A fellow said to me some time ago concerning the church, "I would just as soon go out and play golf on Sunday." Knowing the church he attended, I understood how he felt. In fact, I believe he could be more spiritual out on the golf course than he could be in a service in that church. The point is that he should find a church that is really preaching *Christ*. Oh, how wonderful He is! How important it is to have a *personal* relationship to Him.

For they being ignorant of God's righteousness, and going about to establish their own righteousness, have not submitted themselves unto the righteousness of God [Rom. 10:3].

This was true of Israel, and it is true of the average church member today. Dr. Griffith Thomas commented on this lack of discernment. "Is it not marvellous that people can read the Bible and all the time fail to see its essential teaching and its personal application to themselves? There is scarcely anything more surprising and saddening than the presence of intellectual knowledge of God's Word with an utter failure to appreciate its spiritual meaning and force." I have seen men, officers of the church, who carry such big Bibles under their arms that they leaned in that direction when they walked down the street. I watched them for twenty-one years and saw no spiritual growth. They just did not grow. They had no discernment whatsoever. So many church people have no real discernment of what it really means to be saved.

> **For Christ is the end of the law for righteousness to every one that believeth [Rom. 10:4].**

"Christ is the end of the law" means He is the *goal*. Our Lord made it clear. He said in effect, "I didn't come to patch up an old garment; I came to give you a new garment—the robe of My righteousness" (see Matt. 9:16). The Mosaic Law was given to lead men to Christ; it wasn't given to save men. Paul said to the Galatian believers that ". . . the law was our schoolmaster to bring us unto Christ, that we might be justified by faith" (Gal. 3:24). The Law was not given to save us, but to show us that we needed to be saved. It takes us by the hand, brings us to the Cross of Christ, and says, "Little fellow, you need a Savior." The Law came to an end in Christ. "Christ is become of no effect unto you, whosoever of you are justified by the law; ye are fallen from grace" (Gal. 5:4). William R. Newell (*Romans Verse by Verse*, p. 393) made the statement: "The Law is no more a rule of life than it is a means of righteousness." It is for *everyone* that *believes*, which suggests both the freeness and universality of salvation. "Everyone"— universal. "Believeth"—oh, the freeness of it! Why don't you accept it?

PRESENT STANDING OF ISRAEL

For Moses describeth the righteousness which is of the law, That the man which doeth those things shall live by them [Rom. 10:5].

Granted that you could attain a righteousness in the law, it would be your *own* righteousness, not God's righteousness. It could never measure up to His.

> **But the righteousness which is of faith speaketh on this wise, Say not in thine heart, Who shall ascend into heaven? (that is, to bring Christ down from above:) [Rom. 10:6].**

He talks about ascending up to heaven to bring it down, or going down to hell and bringing it up. My friend, the righteousness that Paul is talking about—he quotes from Deuteronomy 30:11–14—is *available!*

> **Or, Who shall descend into the deep? (that is, to bring up Christ again from the dead.) [Rom. 10:7].**

You don't have to make a trip anywhere to get it.

life & death is in the tongue

> **But what saith it? The word is nigh thee, even in thy mouth, and in thy heart: that is, the word of faith, which we preach [Rom. 10:8].**

It is available right where you are sitting. A great many folk think they have to go to an altar in some sort of meeting to be saved. But salvation is available to you right where you are now.

> **That if thou shalt confess with thy mouth the Lord Jesus, and shalt believe in thine heart that God hath raised him from the dead, thou shalt be saved.**

a child of God is never not defeated

For with the heart man believeth unto righteousness; and with the mouth confession is made unto salvation [Rom. 10:9–10].

Use the word of God. *I am the greatest.*
       Claim the victory

There are many folk who maintain that a believer has to make a public confession of faith. That is not what Paul is saying here. It does not mean to go forward in a public meeting. In the church I served for twenty-one years I saw many people come forward, but they were not all saved. Paul is not saying that you have to make a public confession.

Paul is saying that man needs to bring into agreement his confession and his life. The mouth and the heart should be in harmony, saying the same thing. It is with the heart that you believe. Your "heart" means your total personality, your entire being. You see, there are some folk who say something with their mouths—they give lip service to God—but their hearts are far from Him. When you make a public confession, you be dead sure that your heart is right along with you; that you are not just saying idle words that mean nothing to you personally. If there is confession without faith, it is due either to self-deception or to hypocrisy. If there is faith without confession, it may be cowardice. It seems to me that Paul is saying here that James is accurate, ". . . faith without works is dead" (James 2:20). If you are going to work your mouth, be sure you have faith in your heart, my friend.

"Believe in thine heart that God hath raised him from the dead" means that the resurrection of Christ is the heart of the gospel. As Paul said earlier, He "was delivered for our offences, and was raised again for our justification" (Rom. 4:25).

For the scripture saith, Whosoever believeth on him shall not be ashamed [Rom. 10:11].

      means discipline

Paul is quoting from Isaiah 28:16: "Therefore thus saith the Lord God, Behold, I lay in Zion for a foundation a stone, a tried stone, a precious corner stone, a sure foundation: he that believeth shall not make haste." The difference in our translation is not due to Paul's changing the quotation. Rather, the word for *confound* and *make haste* is the same. It means to flee because of fear. Paul is quoting Isaiah to enforce his previous statement that the "by faith righteousness" is taught in other passages in the Old Testament. This passage also shows the universal character of salvation in the word *whosoever*.

Hope
Harmony

> **For there is no difference between the Jew and the Greek: for the same Lord over all is rich unto all that call upon him [Rom. 10:12].**

There is no distinction between the Jew and the Greek (or Gentile)—all have sinned and come short of the glory of God. All, if they are to be saved, must come the same way to Christ. The Lord Jesus said, ". . . no man cometh unto the Father, but by me" (John 14:6). You can't come to Him by the Old Testament ritual or by the Mosaic Law. Salvation is offered to all people on the same basis of mercy—by faith. Hear and believe the gospel.

The best that I can under the circonstance

PRESENT SALVATION FOR BOTH JEW AND GENTILE

> **For whosoever shall call upon the name of the Lord shall be saved [Rom. 10:13].**

Breaking the law

This is a remarkable statement, which Paul draws from the Old Testament (see Joel 2:32), to enforce his argument that salvation is by faith. This makes it very clear that both Jew and Gentile are to call on the Lord. To "call upon the name of the Lord" means to believe in the Lord Jesus Christ.

no
Excuses

Through grace + mercy
not by works

> **How then shall they call on him in whom they have not believed? and how shall they believe in him of whom they have not heard? and how shall they hear without a preacher?** 3

> **And how shall they preach, except they be sent? as it is written, How beautiful are the feet of them that preach the gospel of peace, and bring glad tidings of good things! [Rom. 10:14–15].**

These excuses will not hold water.
Sent the prophets to preach to the jews.

It is necessary to understand Paul's position in order to appreciate these verses. The Jews, his own people, hated the apostle Paul even though they applauded Saul, the Pharisee. He is showing the logic of his position. They rejected his claim, or the right of any of the apostles, to proclaim a gospel that omitted the Mosaic system which had degenerated into Pharisaism.

Paul shows that there must be messengers of the gospel who have credentials from God. Paul, you recall, began this epistle with the claim that he was a called apostle of Jesus Christ (see Rom. 1:1). There follows a logical sequence. Preachers must be sent in order for people to hear that they might believe, for they would not know how to call upon God. Paul pinpoints all on *believing*. This, therefore, necessitated his ministry.

Paul clinches this bit of logic with a quotation from Isaiah 52:7 which says: "How beautiful upon the mountains are the feet of him that bringeth good tidings, that publisheth peace; that bringeth good tidings of good, that publisheth salvation; that saith unto Zion, Thy God reigneth!" This quotation precedes the marvelous fifty-third chapter of Isaiah, which is a prophecy of Christ's death and resurrection. He opened it with the prophet's query, ". . . Who hath believed our report? . . ." (Isa. 53:1). The law of Moses surely was not glad tidings of good things, but it was a ministration of death.

We are told here that the feet of those who bear glad tidings are beautiful. I believe that my radio program is important, and I am giving the rest of my life to it. I feel it is important to get God's Word out to needy people. One day I was making tapes for the program in my bare feet. I looked at them and concluded that they are not beautiful. There is nothing about feet that causes them to be an object of beauty. But God calls beautiful the feet of His called-ones and His sent-messengers—beautiful. John Peter Lange has an appropriate word on this: "In their running and hastening, in their scaling obstructing mountains, they are the symbols of the earnestly-desired, winged movement and appearance of the Gospel itself." That is one of the reasons I love the opportunity provided by radio today. We can scale mountains, go over the plains, reach over the vast expanses of water, and go into the inner recesses of the earth with the gospel. We can go

into homes, automobiles, and places of business. We have been even
in barrooms with the gospel by radio. It is wonderful to get out the
Word of God. It is wonderful to have feet that the Lord calls beautiful!

> **But they have not all obeyed the gospel. For Esaias saith,
> Lord, who hath believed our report? [Rom. 10:16].**

While we are amazed at the great number of folk who tell us that they
have received Christ because of our ministry, when we look at the total
picture, it is a very small minority. Who *has* believed our report? Not
very many.

> **So then faith cometh by hearing, and hearing by the
> word of God [Rom. 10:17].**

Oh, this is so important! Fai h does not come by preaching philosophy or psychology or some political nostrum; it comes by preaching
the *Word of God*. Until you hear the Word of God, you cannot be saved,
my friend.

> **But I say, Have they not heard? Yes verily, their sound
> went into all the earth, and their words unto the ends of
> the world [Rom. 10:18].**

While I am not saying that Paul has reference to radio, it certainly
applies to radio broadcasting. Radio is a marvelous way of getting
God's Word to the ends of the world.

> **But I say, Did not Israel know? First Moses saith, I will
> provoke you to jealousy by them that are no people, and
> by a foolish nation I will anger you [Rom. 10:19].**

Paul is quoting from Deuteronomy 32:21. Today God is calling out a
people from among Gentiles. Paul will develop this thought in the
next chapter.

**But Esaias is very bold, and saith, I was found of them
that sought me not; I was made manifest unto them that
asked not after me [Rom. 10:20].**

Paul quotes from Isaiah 65:1: "I am sought of them that asked not for
me; I am found of them that sought me not: I said, Behold me, behold
me, unto a nation that was not called by my name." Even Isaiah pre-
dicted gentile salvation. The Gentiles in darkness were finding
Christ. What excuse could Israel who had the Old Testament Scriptures offer? They are entirely without excuse.

**But to Israel he saith, All day long I have stretched forth
my hands unto a disobedient and gainsaying people
[Rom. 10:21].**

Have you ever stopped to think how tiresome it is to hold your hands
out for a long period of time? Try it sometime and see how long you
can do it. It is one of the most tiring things in the world. When Moses
held up his hands in prayer to God for Israel's victory in battle, Aaron
and Hur had to prop up his hands because he got so tired holding
them up (see Exod. 17:9–12). But God says, "I have been holding out
My hands to a disobedient people" (see Isa. 65:2). No one knows how
gracious God has been to the nation Israel.

Stephen's final word to this nation is revealing: "Ye stiffnecked
and uncircumcised in heart and ears, ye do always resist the Holy
Ghost: as your fathers did, so do ye. Which of the prophets have not
your fathers persecuted? and they have slain them which shewed before of the coming of the Just One; of whom ye have been now the
betrayers and murderers: Who have received the law by the disposi-
tion of angels, and have not kept it" (Acts 7:51–53). This is not confined to Israel. It could be said today that God is holding out His hands
to a gainsaying world. I marvel at the patience of God. I do not mean
to be irreverant, but if I were running the show on this little earth
down here, I would make a lot of changes. I would move in like a
bulldozer! But God is just holding out His hands to our gainsaying
world.

CHAPTER 11

THEME: Remnant of Israel finding salvation; remainder of Israel blinded; reason for setting aside the nation Israel; restoration of the nation Israel; reason for restoring the nation Israel

We will see that God has a future purpose with Israel. In chapter 9 we saw God's *past* dealings with Israel. In chapter 10 we saw God's *present* dealings with Israel: a remnant of Israel is finding salvation. Perhaps you are saying, "Well, it must be a very small remnant." It is larger than you might think it is. It is estimated that there are about fifteen million Jews throughout the world, and the percentage of those who are believers is probably much higher than that of the gentile world with its four billion people.

We have seen that the nation rejected Christ and the "by faith" righteousness of God in Christ which was offered to them. And now God has rejected them temporarily as a nation. Two questions naturally arise: Has God permanently rejected them as a nation? In other words, does the nation of Israel have a future? Secondly, are all the promises of the Old Testament nullified by the rejection of Israel? Remember that God had promised primacy to Israel in the Old Testament. He had said they would be the head, not the tail, of the nations (see Deut. 28:13). My friend, all the promises of the Old Testament will have a literal fulfillment. Paul will make that clear.

REMNANT OF ISRAEL FINDING SALVATION

I say then, Hath God cast away his people? God forbid. For I also am an Israelite, of the seed of Abraham, of the tribe of Benjamin [Rom. 11:1].

What people is Paul talking about? *Israel.* In case the amillennialist might miss this, Paul is very specific. Paul himself is present proof. He is a true Israelite of genuine stock. He is descended from Abraham;

he is from one of the twelve tribes of Israel, Benjamin, one of the two
tribes that never seceded from the nation. He was 100 percent Israelite.

"God forbid" is more accurately, *Let it not be!* It is a strong negative. Even the form of the question demands a negative answer. God
has not cast away Israel as a nation.

> **God hath not cast away his people which he foreknew.
> Wot ye not what the scripture saith of Elias? how he
> maketh intercession to God against Israel, saying,**

> **Lord, they have killed thy prophets, and digged down
> thine altars; and I am left alone, and they seek my life
> [Rom. 11:2–3].**

Paul uses old Elijah as an illustration, and he makes a good one. Elijah
stood for God, and he stood alone. How I admire that man standing
alone for God against 450 prophets of Baal. And Elijah goes to the
Lord to complain. He says, "Lord, I am all alone; I am the only one
left." God says, "Wait a minute, you think you are alone, but you are
not."

> **But what saith the answer of God unto him? I have re-
> served to myself seven thousand men, who have not
> bowed the knee to the image of Baal [Rom. 11:4].**

Elijah was totally unaware that God had been working in the hearts of
seven thousand men. If there were seven thousand men who had not
bowed the knee to Baal, then it follows that there were about twice as
many women who did not bow the knee either, if you go by percent-
ages. For the northern kingdom this was a sizable remnant in the day
of Ahab and Jezebel.

> **Even so then at this present time also there is a remnant
> according to the election of grace [Rom. 11:5].**

God always had a remnant in Israel. That remnant today is composed of those Jews who have come to Christ. This is the reason Paul will say later that all Israel is not Israel.

> **And if by grace, then is it no more of works: otherwise grace is no more grace. But if it be of works, then is it no more grace: otherwise work is no more work [Rom. 11:6].**

In other words, grace and works represent two mutually exclusive systems. They are diametrically opposed to each other. The remnant at this time is composed of those who are not saved by works or by merit; they are saved by the grace of God. The future purpose of God—from the day Paul wrote down to the present—concerns those who will accept Christ.

What about those who do not accept Christ? Well, the remainder of Israel is hardened.

REMAINDER OF ISRAEL BLINDED

It is important to notice that they were hardened because they failed; they did not fail because they were hardened. A lot of folk get the cart before the horse—in fact, they get the horse in the cart, and it doesn't belong there!

> **What then? Israel hath not obtained that which he seeketh for; but the election hath obtained it, and the rest were blinded [Rom. 11:7].**

Did they fail to come to Christ because they had been blinded? Oh, no. They had been exposed to the gospel as no other people have been exposed to it. God said, "All day long have I stretched forth my hands unto a disobedient and gainsaying people" (Rom. 10:21). He has been patient with them. Now they are blinded because they would not accept the light He gave them.

(According as it is written, God hath given them the spirit of slumber, eyes that they should not see, and ears that they should not hear;) unto this day [Rom. 11:8].

They had rejected, you see. When a man rejects, he becomes the most difficult to reach with the grace of God.

And David saith, Let their table be made a snare, and a trap, and a stumblingblock, and a recompence unto them [Rom. 11:9].

This is a quotation from Psalm 69:22 which says, "Let their table become a snare before them: and that which should have been for their welfare, let it become a trap." The table has reference to feasting, which is representative of material prosperity. The children of Israel had great feasts at which they were actually guests of God—they did not invite God to their feasts as the pagans did—rather, God invited them. The Passover was a notable example. The thought here is that they were feasting in a conceited confidence which was entirely pagan. Their carnal security deceived them as to their true spiritual ruin. They trusted the things they ate without any true confidence in God. My friend, this is the condition at the present moment of multitudes of church members. They come to the Lord's Supper without a spiritual understanding.

Let their eyes be darkened that they may not see, and bow down their back alway [Rom. 11:10].

God gives light in order that men might see, but if they are blind, they will not see. The light reveals the blindness of multitudes today. I am amazed that so many intelligent people do not seem to understand what the Bible is all about.

REASON FOR SETTING ASIDE THE NATION ISRAEL

The nation Israel was set aside for the salvation of the Gentiles. Paul deals with this in the following section.

> **I say then, Have they stumbled that they should fall?
> God forbid: but rather through their fall salvation is
> come unto the Gentiles, for to provoke them to jealousy
> [Rom. 11:11].**

In other words: I say then, did they stumble in order that they might fall? Away with the thought—that's not it. But by their false step, salvation has come to the Gentiles, to provoke Israel to jealousy.

Now Paul opens this verse with the same engaging inquiry as he did verse 1. Do you remember that he raised the question, "Hath God cast away his people?" (v. 1). Rejection is only partial and temporary. His question is, "Have they stumbled in such a way that they will not rise again?" The answer is an emphatic negative. Their fall has enabled God through His providence to open the gates of salvation *wide* to the Gentiles. The Jew will see the reality of salvation of the Gentiles, that they are experiencing the blessings of God which the Jew thought could come only to him. This should move him to emulation, not jealousy as we define it. In our trips to Israel, we have had several guides who were Jewish. They were puzzled that we were so interested in things that are Jewish in the nation Israel. They marveled at that. I have visited other countries and enjoyed them. I enjoyed England because some of my ancestors came from that area. In Egypt I saw the pyramids and that great hunk of rock there, and now that I have seen it, I don't want to see it again. But I have an interest in Israel that is not equaled in any other nation. The Jewish people don't understand this. One Jewish guide talked to me about it. He said, "I want to know why these things are so important to you."

> **Now if the fall of them be the riches of the world, and the
> diminishing of them the riches of the Gentiles; how
> much more their fulness? [Rom. 11:12].**

Israel has been set aside; that is, God is not dealing with them as a nation at this time. When God does begin to deal with them, they won't have any problem with the Arab—that conflict will be completely resolved. Israel will not live in fear, because God has made it very clear that every man is going to dwell in peace and tranquility. "But they shall sit every man under his vine and under his fig tree; and none shall make them afraid: for the mouth of the LORD of hosts hath spoken it" (Mic. 4:4).

Now since their setting aside has brought the grace of God to Gentiles, what about the grace of God toward the Gentiles after the Jews are received again? It will be multiplied. James made this clear at that great council at Jerusalem. He said that God is calling out from among Gentiles a people for His name just as He is calling out Israelites. Then God says, "After this I will return, and will build again the tabernacle of David, which is fallen down; and I will build again the ruins thereof, and I will set it up: that the residue of men might seek after the Lord, and all the Gentiles, upon whom my name is called, saith the Lord, who doeth all these things" (Acts 15:16–17). This is my reason for periodically making a statement—that sometimes puzzles folk—that the greatest "revival" took place on this earth before the church got here. (I use the word *revival* in the popular sense of a turning to God.) A man by the name of Jonah went into the city of Ninevah and saw the entire city turn to God. It is true that there was a great turning to God on the Day of Pentecost (which marks the beginning of the church), but what was the percentage? Pentecost was a feast in Jerusalem to which all male Israelites were required to go—there must have been several hundred thousand Jews in the environs of Jerusalem. How many were saved? Well, judging from the record, there were probably about ten thousand who were saved after the first few days of preaching. That is actually a small percentage. And the greatest revival since then took place in the Hawaiian Islands. The percentage there was probably 50 percent. But that was small in comparison to the days of Jonah. And I believe that the greatest revival will take place after the church leaves this earth. Actually, the church has not done too well. I believe that after the church has been raptured, multitudes of Gentiles will turn to God—not only in the Great Tribulation period, but in the Millennium. Gentile nations will enter the Millennium, and a great many of them are going to like the rule of Christ, and they will turn to God during that period. I believe this with all my heart.

For I speak to you Gentiles, inasmuch as I am the apostle of the Gentiles, I magnify mine office:

If by any means I may provoke to emulation them which are my flesh, and might save some of them [Rom. 11:13–14].

Perhaps my translation will help you in the understanding of these two verse: "But I speak to you, the Gentiles. Inasmuch, then, as I [Paul] am an apostle of Gentiles, I glorify my ministry, if by any means I may move to emulation, that is, provoke to jealousy them of my flesh, and may save some of them."

In other words, Paul says, in effect, "I am an apostle to the Gentiles, and I rejoice in that. But as I preach to the Gentiles, I hope it will move many of my own people to turn to Christ also." Paul, you remember, wrote to the Corinthians, "And unto the Jews I became as a Jew, that I might gain the Jews; to them that are under the law, as under the law, that I might gain them that are under the law" (1 Cor. 9:20).

This is the reason Paul went to Jerusalem with his head shaven and under an oath—he was trying to win his people to Christ. Should he have done this since he lived under grace? Living under grace means that he could do it if he wanted to. In his letter to the Corinthians he continued, "To them that are without law, as without law, (being not without law to God, but under the law to Christ,) that I might gain them that are without law" (1 Cor. 9:21). In other words, he was obeying Christ. Then Paul says, "To the weak became I as weak, that I might gain the weak: I am made all things to all men, that I might by all means save some" (1 Cor. 9:22). He was first of all fulfilling his office as an apostle to the Gentiles, and in so doing, he was trying to move his Jewish brethren to turn to Christ. Some turned to Christ— only a few—but some. In all of this Paul was fulfilling his ministry, and God was accomplishing His purpose in this age with both Jew and Gentile.

I understand the satisfaction Paul felt in doing what God had called him to do. God has a place for you, my friend. He may want you to get busy and teach a Sunday school class, do personal work, or reach people through a business enterprise. Or He may want you to support another who is really getting out the Word of God. Whatever it is, you will experience great satisfaction in doing what you are confident God has called you to do.

> **For if the casting away of them be the reconciling of the world, what shall the receiving of them be, but life from the dead? [Rom. 11:15].**

It is wonderful to anticipate the future. I think the greatest days are ahead of us. From man's point of view, the future is dark. Man has gotten his world in a mess. I felt sorry for a businessman to whom I was talking in Hawaii. We started chatting on the golf course. He told me that he was a businessman from Chicago—a vice-president of some concern. Obviously he had money, but, oh, how pessimistic he was about the future. Many thinking people are very pessimistic about the future of our civilization. But my God is on the throne, and He is going to straighten it out. The greatest days are yet in the future. Oh, the glorious future a child of God has. If I were not a dignified preacher, I would say *Hallelujah!*

> **For if the firstfruit be holy, the lump is also holy: and if the root be holy, so are the branches [Rom. 11:16].**

You may recall that in the Book of Numbers, God said, "Of the first of your dough ye shall give unto the LORD an heave offering in your generations" (Num. 15:21). "Dough," of course, is bread dough! A part of the dough was offered to God as a token that all of it was acceptable.

The "firstfruit" evidently refers to the origin of the nation: Abraham, Isaac, and Jacob.

"Holy" has no reference to any moral quality, but to the fact that it was set apart for God. Now if the firstfruit, or the first dough—that little bit of dough—was set apart for God, what about the whole harvest? Since Abraham, Isaac, and Jacob were set apart for God, what about the nation? It all belongs to God, you see. God is not through with the nation Israel.

> **And if some of the branches be broken off, and thou, being a wild olive tree, wert grafted in among them, and with them partakest of the root and fatness of the olive tree [Rom. 11:17].**

You and I benefit because of the nation Israel. That is the reason I could never be anti–Semitic. I owe too much to them as a nation.

> **Boast not against the branches. But if thou boast, thou bearest not the root, but the root thee.**

> **Thou wilt say then, The branches were broken off, that I might be grafted in [Rom. 11:18–19].**

The "olive tree" is a picture of the nation Israel, and the "wild olive" is the church. Everything you and I have is rooted in the fact that God called Abraham, Isaac, and Jacob and that out of the nation Israel He brought Jesus Christ, our Savior and our Lord.

> **Well; because of unbelief they were broken off, and thou standest by faith. Be not highminded, but fear [Rom. 11:20].**

The important thing is that they were set aside because of their unbelief. Oh, my Christian friend, you do not stand before God on your merit, your church membership, or your good life. You stand on one basis alone: your faith in Jesus Christ.

Now Paul gives a word of warning.

> **For if God spared not the natural branches, take heed lest he also spare not thee [Rom. 11:21].**

Since God did not spare the nation Israel when they apostatized, the argument is that He will not spare an apostate church. I am more and more convinced that the church which is based on a philosophy or ritual or some sort of gyroflection—the type of church which was designated in the third chapter of the Book of Revelation as the church of Laodicea—will go into the Great Tribulation. As Dr. George Gill used to say, "Some churches will meet on the Sunday morning after the Rapture, and they won't miss a member." That's Laodicea.

In contrast to this, He says to the church of Philadelphia, "Because thou hast kept the word of my patience, I also will keep thee from the hour of temptation [that is, the Tribulation], which shall come upon all the world, to try them that dwell upon the earth" (Rev. 3:10). He promised to keep from the Tribulation that church which has an open door before it and is getting out the Word of God. My friend, I belong to that church; I hope you do also. It is an invisible body of believers. This is the church that will be taken to meet Christ at the time of the Rapture, which precedes the Great Tribulation.

RESTORATION OF THE NATION ISRAEL

Now we shall see that the restoration of the nation Israel will bring the greatest blessing.

> **Behold therefore the goodness and severity of God: on them which fell, severity; but toward thee, goodness, if thou continue in his goodness: otherwise thou also shalt be cut off [Rom. 11:22].**

These are stern words. Paul calls upon the Gentiles to behold two examples. Rejected Israel reveals the severity of God, but to the Gentiles who have turned to God, the benevolent goodness of God is revealed. These two sides of God need to be revealed today: the judgment of God against the rejection of Christ against sin, and the grace of God to those that will trust Christ.

Paul did not have the complete picture of the severity of God toward Israel. The history of Israel in the destruction of Jerusalem in

A.D. 70 and all that succeeded it is a terrifying story. My friend, let's not trifle with the grace of God. It is grace which has brought us into the family of God and granted us so many privileges. After over nineteen hundred years the gentile church is as much a failure, if not more so, than Israel.

> **And they also, if they abide not still in unbelief, shall be grafted in: for God is able to graft them in again [Rom. 11:23].**

Since God accepted Gentiles who had no merit, surely God can restore Israel who likewise has no merit.

"Again" is the key word. God will again restore Israel. The Old Testament makes it very clear that Israel is going to turn to God again. As an example, read Jeremiah 23:3–8, which is one of the many remarkable prophecies of the restoration of Israel. Zechariah speaks of this: "And I will pour upon the house of David, and upon the inhabitants of Jerusalem, the spirit of grace and of supplications: and they shall look upon me whom they have pierced, and they shall mourn for him, as one mourneth for his only son, and shall be in bitterness for him, as one that is in bitterness for his firstborn" (Zech. 12:10). This will be the great Day of Atonement. They will turn to God in repentance, and God will save them just as He saves us—by His marvelous, infinite mercy and grace.

> **For if thou wert cut out of the olive tree which is wild by nature, and wert grafted contrary to nature into a good olive tree: how much more shall these, which be the natural branches, be grafted into their own olive tree? [Rom. 11:24].**

Paul continues the illustration of the olive tree. The olive tree is Israel with Abraham as the root. Some of the branches were cut off. The nation, as such, was rejected. God grafted in Gentiles, but not by their becoming Jewish proselytes, which would mean they would have to adopt the Old Testament ritual. Rather, He cut off Israel and grafted in the church—including both Jew and Gentile—directly and immediately upon Abraham by faith. If God could and did do that, it is reasonable to conclude that He can and will take the natural branches and graft them in again. In other words, He will not cast Israel away permanently.

> **For I would not, brethren, that ye should be ignorant of this mystery, lest ye should be wise in your own conceits; that blindness in part is happened to Israel, until the fulness of the Gentiles be come in [Rom. 11:25].**

"The fulness of the Gentiles" began with the calling out of the church. "Simeon hath declared how God at the first did visit the Gentiles, to take out of them a people for his name" (Acts 15:14). It will continue until the rapture of the church. Blindness and hardening of Israel will continue as long as the church is present in the world.

The word *mystery* needs a word of explanation. In the ancient world of Paul's day there were mystery religions. Today it applies in a popular way to a story that has an unrevealed plot or person. It is used in Scripture in neither of these ways. In the New Testament the word is used to refer to that which had been concealed but is now revealed. The mystery here is the identification of the fullness of the Gentiles, which was not a subject of revelation in the Old Testament.

> **And so all Israel shall be saved: as it is written, There shall come out of Sion the Deliverer, and shall turn away ungodliness from Jacob:**
>
> **For this is my covenant unto them, when I shall take away their sins [Rom. 11:26–27].**

When Paul says "all Israel shall be saved," he does not mean every individual Israelite will be saved. It is the *nation* he has before us in this chapter. In every age, only a remnant is saved. The quotation Paul uses is from Isaiah 59:20 in the Old Testament: "And the Redeemer shall come to Zion, and unto them that turn from transgression in

Jacob, saith the LORD." The message to the individual is that he will have to "turn from transgression" to the Lord. There will be a remnant that will turn to Him. All of *them* will be saved. He speaks of the saved remnant as the nation Israel.

There is always only a remnant that is saved. There was a remnant in Elijah's day; there was a remnant in David's day; there was a remnant in Paul's day; there is a remnant in our day; and there will be a remnant during the Great Tribulation period.

> **As concerning the gospel, they are enemies for your sakes: but as touching the election, they are beloved for the fathers' sakes.**
>
> **For the gifts and calling of God are without repentance [Rom. 11:28–29].**

In other words, with reference to the gospel, they are enemies for your sakes; but with reference to the election, they are beloved for the sake of the fathers. For the gifts of grace and the calling of God are without repentance—without a change of mind. Paul is summing up the preceding discussion. There have been two lines of thought which are seemingly in conflict and contradictory, although both are true. In the first place, Israel is regarded as an enemy for the sake of the Gentiles— that is, so the gospel can go to the Gentiles. On the other hand, they are beloved for the sake of Abraham, Isaac, and Jacob. Therefore, a Christian cannot indulge in any form of anti–Semitism—that is a point I have made before, and continue to make it.

The failure of Israel and our failure likewise do not alter the plan and purpose of God.

"The gifts" are not natural gifts, but the word has to do with grace.

The "calling" is not an invitation, but it is the effectual calling of God, which is "without repentance." In other words, God is not asking even repentance from an unsaved person. The "calling of God" does not require any human movement. From God's viewpoint it is without man's repentance or change of mind. Some folk think they have to shed tears in order to be saved. Now certainly the shedding of tears could be a by-product of an emotional person who turns to Christ, but the tears have nothing in the world to do with your salvation. It is your faith in Christ that saves you. And neither is your faith meritorious. It is Christ who is meritorious. Your faith enables you to lay hold of Him.

> **For as ye in times past have not believed God, yet have now obtained mercy through their unbelief:**
>
> **Even so have these also now not believed, that through your mercy they also may obtain mercy [Rom. 11:30–31].**

You see, Paul is writing to Gentiles—the church in Rome was largely composed of Gentile believers. By this time, many Gentiles were being saved. He is drawing a contrast here between the nation of Israel and the Gentiles. In times past, the Gentiles did not believe, but now a remnant of the Gentiles have "obtained mercy." During this same time period Israel as a nation, which formerly believed, does not now believe. Paul puts down the principle by which God saves both Jew and Gentile: it is by mercy. Just as God showed mercy to the Gentiles, He will show mercy to the nation Israel.

> **For God hath concluded them all in unbelief, that he might have mercy upon all [Rom. 11:32].**

Both Jew and Gentile are in the stubborn state of rebellion and aggravated unbelief. Because of this, by *grace* we are saved, through faith; and that not of ourselves, it is the gift of God; not of works, lest any of us should boast (see Eph. 2:8–9).

REASON FOR RESTORING THE NATION ISRAEL

What is the reason that the nation Israel will be restored? Well, that is locked in the riches of the wisdom of God. My friend, let's rest on the fact that what God is doing is wise, it is right, and it is the best that can be done. You and I have an old nature that questions God when He makes a decision. I have heard many Christians say, "Why are the heathen lost when they haven't heard the gospel? God has no right to condemn them!" My friend, God has every right imaginable. He is God. And what He is doing is right. If you don't think it is right, your thinking is wrong. And if you don't think He is being smart, you are wrong. God is not stupid. You and I may be stupid, but God is not. Oh, how we need to recognize this!

> **O the depth of the riches both of the wisdom and knowl-
> edge of God! how unsearchable are his judgments, and
> his ways past finding out! [Rom. 11:33].**

Paul has come to the place of recognizing the wisdom and the glory of all that he has been discussing.

Godet's statement on this section is worth quoting: "Like a traveller who has reached the summit of an Alpine ascent, the apostle turns and contemplates. Depths are at his feet, but waves of light illumine them, and there spreads all around an immense horizon which his eye commands."

This section is pure praise and is no argument at all, yet it is the greatest argument of all. If we do not understand the *why* of God's dealings with Israel, with the Gentiles, and with ourselves, it is not because there is not a good and sufficient reason. The difficulty is with our inability to comprehend the wisdom and ways of God. "But the natural man receiveth not the things of the Spirit of God: for they are foolishness unto him: neither can he know them, because they are spiritually discerned" (1 Cor. 2:14).

Once, while driving back from Texas to California, my little girl developed a fever of 104 degrees. I took her to a hospital in Phoenix, Arizona. She did not understand why I had taken her to the hospital, especially when the doctor probed around and actually made her cry. She said, "Daddy, why did you bring me here?" She did not understand that, since she was sick, I was doing the wisest thing I could do under the circumstances and that I was doing it because I loved her. Oh, my friend, God is doing what is best for us. We may not under-

stand the things that happen to us, but we must believe that it is for
our good that God allows them. We are like little children, and we
cannot understand God's ways. Our circumstances may not always
seem to be good, but they come from the "depth of the riches both of
the wisdom and knowledge of God." God says to us, "For my thoughts
are not your thoughts, neither are your ways my ways, saith the LORD.
For as the heavens are higher than the earth, so are my ways higher
than your ways, and my thoughts than your thoughts" (Isa. 55:8–9).
Oh, how we need to recognize this fact.

> **For who hath known the mind of the Lord? or who hath
> been his counsellor?**
>
> **Or who hath first given to him, and it shall be recom-
> pensed unto him again? [Rom. 11:34–35].**

These questions that we have here are simple enough, but the answer
is not so easy.

"Who hath known the mind of the Lord?" Well, no one knows the
mind of the Lord—that's the answer. It was Paul's ambition to know
Him. He says, "That I may know him, and the power of his resurrection, and the fellowship of his sufferings, being made conformable
unto his death" (Phil. 3:10).

"Who hath been his counsellor?" No one can advise God. I have
seen a lot of church boards that felt they were really giving God good
advice, but He doesn't need it. Have you noticed that the Lord Jesus
never asked for advice when He was here on earth? One time—before
feeding the five thousand—He asked Philip, ". . . Whence shall we
buy bread, that these may eat?" Why did He ask that question? "And
this he said to prove him: for he himself knew what he would do"
(John 6:5–6). He didn't need Philip's advice. The fact of the matter is,
he didn't use His disciples' advice. They said, "Send them away." He
said, "You give them something to eat." My friend, God does not ask
for advice, although a lot of folk want to give Him advice today.

"Who hath first given to him?" Have you ever really given anything to God which put Him in the awkward position of owing you

something? If you were able to give God something, He would owe you something. What do you have that He hasn't already given you? I think one reason many of us are so poor is simply because we return to Him so little of what He has given us. To tell the truth, God says He won't be in debt to anybody. When somebody gives Him something, He turns around and gives him more. Years ago someone asked a financier in Philadelphia, a wonderful Christian man, "How is it that you have such wealth, and yet you give away so much?" The financier replied, "Well, I shovel it out, and God shovels it in; and God's shovel is bigger than my shovel!" Oh, my friend, most of us are not giving God a chance to use His shovel! We cannot do anything for Him—He will give us back more than we give to Him.

> **For of him, and through him, and to him, are all things: to whom be glory for ever. Amen [Rom. 11:36].**

This just lifts me to the heights. Let me give you my translation: Because out of Him, and through Him, and unto Him are all things. To Him be the glory unto the ages. Amen.

Alford labeled this verse "the sublimest apostrophe existing even in the pages of inspiration itself."

"Out of Him" means God is the all-sufficient cause and source of everything.

"Through Him" means God is the mighty sustainer and worker. ". . . My Father worketh hitherto, and I work," Jesus said (John 5:17).

"Unto Him" means God must call every creature to account to Him. All things flow toward God.

"To whom be glory"—the glory belongs to Him in all ages. Are we robbing God of His glory by taking credit for things we have no business to claim? The glory belongs to Him.

Oh, my friend, what a section of Scripture we have been in, and we leave it reluctantly.

CHAPTER 12

THEME: *Relationship to God; relationship to gifts of the Spirit; relationship to other believers; relationship to unbelievers*

This is the beginning of the final division in the Book of Romans. As you recall, the first eight chapters were doctrinal; the next three chapters were dispensational; now the emphasis in this last section is duty. We come now to the practical application of the theological arguments that Paul has placed before us. Here the gospel walks in shoe leather—and that is where I like it to walk.

In the first part of Romans the reader saw displayed the helmet of salvation and the shield of faith. But in this last section, the feet are shod with the preparation of the gospel of peace. We are to *stand* in the battle; we are to *walk* in our life; we are to *run* in the race.

Someone may suggest that we have already studied the practical application in the section on sanctification. There the gospel walked in shoe leather, it is true, but there is a sharp distinction in these two sections. Under "sanctification" we were dealing with Christian *character*; in this section we are dealing with Christian *conduct*. There it was the *inner* man; here it is the *outward* man. There it was the *condition* of the Christian; here it is the *consecration* of the Christian. There it was who the Christian *is*; here it is what he *does*. We have seen the *privileges* of grace; we now consider the *precepts* of grace. Enunciation of the way of life must be followed by evidences of life. Announcement of justification by faith must be augmented by activity of life.

There is something else we should note as we proceed into this last section. The conduct of the Christian must be expressed in this world by his relationship to those with whom he comes in contact, and these relationships must be regulated in some way. It is so easy to put down rules of conduct, but Paul is not doing that. He has delivered us from the Mosaic Law, and he did not deliver us in order to put us under another legal system. There are a lot of Christians who call themselves separated Christians because they don't do this, they don't do that, and they don't do about fifteen other things. I wish they would *do* something, by the way. I have found that those folk have gossipy tongues—you had better watch them. They ought to recognize that the child of God is *not* given rules and regulations. However, Paul puts down great principles that are to guide the believer. The Holy Spirit is giving the believer a road map of life, showing the curves but not the speed limit. He identifies the motels and eating places which he recommends without commanding the believer to stop at any certain one. Detours are clearly marked, and there is a warning to avoid them. The city of Vanity Fair is named, and the routes of exit are clearly marked. The believer is told to leave without being given the exact route by which to leave—there are several routes.

We are coming down the mountain top of Romans 8—11; we leave the pinnacle of Romans 11:33–36, and we now plunge down to the plane of duty—and it is *plain* duty. This is where we all live and move and have our being.

RELATIONSHIP TO GOD

I beseech you therefore, brethren, by the mercies of God, that ye present your bodies a living sacrifice, holy, acceptable unto God, which is your reasonable service [Rom. 12:1].

In other words: Therefore, I beg of you, brethren, by the mercies of God, that you yield your bodies—your total personalities—a living sacrifice, set apart for God, well-pleasing to God, which is your rational or spiritual service.

Notice that the "therefore" ties it into everything that has come before it. Although it has immediate connection with that which has just preceded it, I am of the opinion that Paul is gathering up the whole epistle when he says, "Therefore."

"I beg of you" is the language of grace, not law. There is no thunder here from Mount Sinai. Moses commanded; Paul exhorts. Could Paul have commanded? Well, he told Philemon that he could have given him a command, but he didn't. Paul doesn't command; he says, "I beg of you."

"By the mercies of God"—the plural is a Hebraism, denoting an abundance of mercy. God is rich in mercy; God has plenty of it, my friend. He has had to use a lot of it for me, but He still has plenty of it for you. "Mercy" means compassion, pity, and the tenderness of God. His compassions never fail.

We are called upon to "present"—to yield. This is the same word we had, you recall, back in chapter 6. Although some expositors suggest that there it refers to the mind while here it refers to the will, I think it is a false distinction. The appeal in both instances is to the will. In the sixth chapter, the way of Christian character is to yield to Him. Here yielding is the way to Christian consecration and conduct.

He says to yield "your bodies," your total personalities. The body is the instrument through which we express ourselves. The mind, the affections, the will, and the Holy Spirit can use the body.

Vincent has assembled the following Scriptures which reveal this wide latitude. We are told to glorify God in our bodies. "For ye are bought with a price: therefore glorify God in your body, and in your spirit, which are God's" (1 Cor. 6:20). "According to my earnest expectation and my hope, that in nothing I shall be ashamed, but that with all boldness, as always, so now also Christ shall be magnified in my body, whether it be by life, or by death" (Phil. 1:20). "Always bearing about in the body the dying of the Lord Jesus, that the life also of Jesus might be made manifest in our body" (2 Cor. 4:10).

By an act of the will we place our total personalities at the disposal of God.

This is our "reasonable service," our rational service, and it is well-pleasing to God.

And be not conformed to this world: but be ye transformed by the renewing of your mind, that ye may prove what is that good, and acceptable, and perfect, will of God [Rom. 12:2].

Kenneth S. Wuest has an excellent translation—actually an interpretation—of this verse: "And stop assuming an outward expression that does not come from within you and is not representative of what you are in your inner being, but is patterned after this age; but change your outward expression to one that comes from within and is representative of your inner being, by the renewing of your mind, resulting in your putting to the test what is the will of God, the good and well-pleasing, and complete will, and having found that it meets specification, placing your approval upon it" (*Romans in the Greek New Testament*, p. 290).

Although this is rather elaborate, it is exactly what Paul is saying in this passage of Scripture. Paul is urging the believer not to fashion his life and conduct by those around him, even those in the church.

I know two or three groups of folk who, when they come together in a meeting, assume a front that is not real at all. They are superpious. Oh, I tell you, when they meet on Sunday night, you would think they had just had their halos shined. They are not normal and they are not natural. Yet if you want to hear the meanest and dirtiest gossip, you meet with that group! The child of God ought not to be like that. We ought to be normal and natural—or probably I should say, normal and supernatural. It is so easy to play a part. That is what the word *hypocrite* really means. *Hupokrites* is the Greek word for actors. They were playing a part. *Hupokrites* means to answer back. In acting it means to get your cue and to say the right thing at the right time. In our daily lives hypocrisy is to seem to be something that we are not. I have learned over the years that some folk who flatter you to your face, smile, and pat you on the back can be your worst enemies. They are dangerous to be with. It was Shakespeare who said something about the world being a stage and that every man must play a part. This is not true of the believer. He must be genuine because the Holy Spirit is working from within, transforming his life by "renewing" the mind.

Again and again Paul calls attention to this. To the Corinthians he said, "But we all, with open face beholding as in a glass the glory of the Lord, are changed into the same image from glory to glory, even as by the Spirit of the Lord" (2 Cor. 3:18). Also to Titus he said, "Not by works of righteousness which we have done, but according to his mercy he saved us, by the washing of regeneration, and renewing of the Holy Ghost" (Titus 3:5).

By permitting the Spirit of God to renew the mind, the believer will be able to test the will of God and find it good. The minute that you and I assume a pose and pretend to be something we are not, it is impossible for us to determine the will of God for our lives. By yielding, the will of God for the life of the believer becomes good and fits the believer's will exactly. It's first good, and then it is acceptable, and finally it is perfect, in that the believer's will and God's will are equal to each other. My friend, you can't improve on that kind of situation. Paul could say, "I can do all things." Where? "Through Christ which strengtheneth me" (Phil 4:13). The believer can do all things that are in God's will. It is wonderful not to have to *act* the part of being Christian, but just be natural and let the Spirit of God move and work through you. Handley C. G. Moule (*The Epistle to the Romans*, p. 335) has put it like this:

> I would not have the restless will
> That hurries to and fro,
> Seeking for some great thing to do
> Or secret thing to know;
> I would be treated as a child,
> And guided where I go.

Oh, to reach the place of just turning this over to the Lord! Paul begs us to do this. This is the way of happiness. This is the way of joy. This is the way of fullness in your life. If you are in a church or in a group of play actors, for God's sake get away from it and try to live a normal Christian life where you can be genuine. A man said to me the other day, "My wife and I have quit going to such and such a group." I asked why. He told me, "We just got tired of going to a place where you almost have to assume something that you are not. Everyone there is being absolutely abnormal. The way I found out was that I had an occasion to meet a super-pious member of the group in a place of business. I hardly recognized the man—his manner and everything about him was different." He was "conformed to the world" when he was not with the pious group. Oh, to be a normal Christian and enjoy God's blessing.

RELATIONSHIP TO GIFTS OF THE SPIRIT

For I say, through the grace given unto me, to every man that is among you, not to think of himself more highly than he ought to think; but to think soberly, according as God hath dealt to every man the measure of faith [Rom. 12:3].

This is my translation: For I am saying through the grace given to me, to everyone among you, not to be thinking of himself more highly than that which is necessary to think, but to think wisely of oneself, even as God has divided a measure of faith to each one.

My translation may have lost something of that pungent statement: "not to think of himself more highly than he ought to think." I imagine that when Paul wrote this, there was a whimsical smile on his face, because there are a great many Christians who are ambitious, who feel that they must have positions of prominence. And I have found out in Christian work that a great many folk in the church want to hold an office. If you want to be a successful pastor today and get a bunch of folk working like termites, you create a great many offices, committees, boards, and have presidents, chairmen, and heads of organizations. You will get a lot of people working who would never work on any other basis. Why? Because they think more highly of themselves than they ought to think.

What we need to do, as Paul says here, is "to think soberly." He says that we ought not try to advance ourselves in Christians circles. There is the ever-present danger of the believer overestimating his ability and his character and his gifts. We need to have a correct estimation of ourselves in relationship to other members of the church.

When I became pastor of certain churches, I was invited to serve as a board member of certain organizations. Finally I was serving on about a dozen or fifteen boards, and I was really a bored member. I was bored for the simple reason that I don't have gifts for that type of thing. To begin with, I don't have the patience to sit and listen to pages of "minutes" that take hours to read. And the second thing is that I just don't like to sit in a board meeting and listen to a group of incompetent men discussing spiritual matters. It took me a long time to find out I didn't have the kind of gift that would make me helpful in such situations, and I was killing myself going to board meetings. The Christian life became a round of being bored. Finally one day I came to myself, like the prodigal son, and I sat down and wrote twelve or more letters of resignation. That was one of the happiest days of my life. And today I am not on anybody's board. I have several friends who say to me, "Oh, won't you be on my board?" I say, "No, I wouldn't help you. I have no gift for it. I'm for you, I'll even pray for you, but I cannot be on your board." My friend, we are not to think of ourselves more highly than we ought to think. We need to recognize our inabilities and do the things God wants us to do. It is a joy to get into the slot where God wants you to be!

> **For as we have many members in one body, and all members have not the same office:**
>
> **So we, being many, are one body in Christ, and every one members one of another [Rom. 12:4–5].**

This is the first time that Paul has introduced the great theme of the church as the body of Christ. This is the primary subject in Paul's letter to the Corinthians, Ephesians, and Colossians. The church as the body of Christ is to function as a body. This means that the many members do not have the same gifts. You may have a gift that I could never exercise. There are many members in the body, hundreds of members, and therefore hundreds of gifts. I do not think Paul ever gave a complete list of all the gifts because every time he dealt with gifts of the Spirit he always brought up new gifts which he had not mentioned in previous lists. I am sure the Spirit of God led him to do that.

**Having then gifts differing according to the grace that is
given to us, whether prophecy, let us prophesy according to the proportion of faith [Rom. 12:6].**

"Gifts" is the Greek word *charismata*, which comes from the same
stem as the word for grace. It can be translated as "grace" or "free gift"
and is what the Spirit of God gives you. He gave to the church men
who had the gift of a prophet, or a teacher, etc.

"Having then gifts"—each member of the body of Christ has a gift
and a function to perform.

"Differing" means that the gifts differ; it does not mean that some
folk do not have a gift. Every individual in the church has a gift. And
the gift is part and parcel of the grace of God to us. When God saves
you and puts you in the body of believers, you are to function. You are
not to function as a machine, but as a member of a body, a living organization. When the gift is exercised, it is confirmed by the power of
the Holy Spirit. Every believer needs to test his gift. If you feel that you
have a certain gift and you are using it, you ought to test it. Analyze
your effectiveness: Are you really a blessing to folk? Are you building
up the church? Or are you dividing the church?

"Prophecy" here does not refer to prediction but to any message
from God. Notice that prophecy is to be done in "proportion" (this is a
mathematical term) to God's provision of the faith and the power to
match the gift.

**Or ministry, let us wait on our ministering: or he that
teacheth, on teaching [Rom. 12:7].**

"Ministering" is performing an act of service, referring to a manifold
ministry with practical implications. There are multitudinous forms
for service in the body of believers which this gift covers—setting up
chairs and giving out songbooks is a ministry. Some folk do not have a
gift of speaking, but they do have a gift of service. I know one dear
lady who can put on a dinner that will make everybody happy. And I
believe in church dinners; if you look at me, you will know I have
been to quite a few of them—and many that this lady put on. That is

her gift, and I've told her that. She would never make a good president of the missionary society, and you wouldn't want her to sing in the choir, but if you want to put on a church dinner for some purpose, she is the one to get. "Ministering" includes many gifts, my friend.

> **Or he that exhorteth, on exhortation: he that giveth, let him do it with simplicity; he that ruleth, with diligence; he that sheweth mercy, with cheerfulness [Rom. 12:8].**

"Exhortation" is the Greek word *paraklésis*, literally "a calling near" or "a calling for." In other words, exhortation is comfort. Some folk have the gift of being able to comfort. I know one pastor who is not a preacher—he knows he is not—but if I were sick or had lost a loved one, he is the man I would want to come to visit me. He can comfort.

"He that giveth" is he that shares his earthly possessions. God may have given you a gift of making money—and that *is* a gift. I know several Christian businessmen who have the Midas touch. That is their gift.

"He that ruleth, with diligence" refers to the gift of leadership. There are certain men who are leaders, and they need to exercise their gift in the church so that everything might be done decently and in order. The business of the church requires a man with the gift of administration.

"He that sheweth mercy" indicates the gift of performing acts of kindness. For instance, there are some believers who can bring a sunbeam into a sickroom, while others cast a spell of gloom.

RELATIONSHIP TO OTHER BELIEVERS

> **Let love be without dissimulation. Abhor that which is evil; cleave to that which is good [Rom. 12:9].**

"Let love be without dissimulation"—that is, without hypocrisy. Don't pat another believer on the back and say something that you don't mean. Let love be without hypocrisy.

"Abhor that which is evil" means to express your hatred of that which is evil. When you find something wrong in the church, bring it to the attention of the proper authorities. If you are on the board of directors and you find things are being done which are not honest, you are to stand up for the truth. There are too many Mr. Milquetoasts and Priscilla Goodbodies, these sweet folk who haven't the intestinal fortitude to stand for that which is honorable. This is the reason many good, fundamental churches are in trouble today. We need men and women with backbone to express their hatred for that which is evil.

"Cleave to that which is good." *Cleave* means to stick like adhesive tape, to be welded or cemented together with the good things. The believer should always be identified with good things rather than shady or questionable practices.

> **Be kindly affectioned one to another with brotherly love; in honour preferring one another;**
>
> **Not slothful in business; fervent in spirit; serving the Lord [Rom. 12:10–11].**

My, how wonderful these things are: have a code of honor, and be aglow with the spirit of God. Never flag in zeal—have a zeal for the things of God.

"Be kindly affectioned one to another with brotherly love." In other words, as to your brotherly love, have family affection one to another. Farrar puts it in this language, "Love the brethren in the faith as though they were brethren in blood." For example, three men are sitting together. Two of the men are identical twins; one twin is a Christian and the other is not. Sitting with these men is a believer from Africa. His culture, background, and language are all different. The color of his skin is different, but he knows the Lord as Savior. The Christian twin is actually closer to the man from Africa than he is to his twin brother. My friend, you ought to be nicer to your fellow believer because you will have to live with him throughout eternity. You had better start getting along now and practice putting up with his peculiar ways. However, he will have a new body then, and he will be rid of his old nature—and you will also! It will make it better for both of you.

"Not slothful in business" is better translated "never flag in zeal." It has nothing to do with business. Luther gives it this translation: "In regard to zeal be not lazy."

"Fervent in spirit," or aglow with the Spirit, suggests that our zeal and enthusiasm should be under the control of the Holy Spirit.

"Serving the Lord" points everything in Christian conduct toward this focal point.

> **Rejoicing in hope; patient in tribulation; continuing instant in prayer;**
>
> **Distributing to the necessity of saints; given to hospitality.**
>
> **Bless them which persecute you: bless, and curse not [Rom. 12:12–14].**

"Rejoicing in hope" should be the portion of the believer. The circumstances of the believer may not warrant rejoicing. The contrary may be true. But he sees the future, and in hope projects himself into other circumstances which are more favorable. I think of a brother down in my Southland years ago. In a church service they were giving favorite Scripture verses. He stood and said that his favorite verse was "It came to pass." Everyone looked puzzled. The preacher stood up and said, "Brother, how in the world can 'It came to pass' be your favorite?" His answer was, "When I have trouble, and when I have problems, I like to read that verse, 'It came to pass,' and I know that my trouble or my problem has come to pass; it hasn't come to stay." He was looking for a new day out there, and that is what Paul has in mind when he says, "rejoicing in hope."

"Continuing instant in prayer" is to be a man or woman of prayer.

"Distributing to the necessity of saints" means sharing the necessities of life with needy believers. A great many churches make a great deal of having a fund for the poor, but how much do they use it? God expects us to share what He has given to us with fellow believers who are in need.

"Given to hospitality" means actually to pursue hospitality. That is, we are to seek out other believers to whom we can extend hospitality. There may be a person in your neighborhood or even in your church who is introverted and retiring yet longs for Christian fellowship. We are to look him up and extend our fellowship to him.

"Bless them which persecute you" seems to be a needless injunction for believers. Surely one believer would not persecute another— or would he? It is difficult to bless a man who is kicking you! But we are to bless and "curse not."

> **Rejoice with them that do rejoice, and weep with them that weep.**
>
> **Be of the same mind one toward another. Mind not high things, but condescend to men of low estate. Be not wise in your own conceits [Rom. 12:15–16].**

"Rejoice with them that do rejoice." The world's motto is "Laugh and the world laughs with you; weep and you weep alone." But that is not true of the believer. We are to enter into the joys and sorrows of other believers. Weep with those who weep.

"Be of the same mind one toward another" doesn't mean uniformity of thought but that we are to have the mind of Christ.

Believers ought to enter emotionally into the lives of other believers. I think that is something that makes genuine Christians so wonderful.

"Mind not high things, but condescend to men of low estate." My friend, let's not be afraid of associating with humble men and things of low estate. Paul said to the Philippians, "Let this mind be in you, which was also in Christ Jesus" (Phil. 2:5)—what kind of a mind did Christ have? A humble mind.

"Be not wise in your own conceits." In other words, stop being wise in your own opinion. What an injunction that is! A great many of the saints think they are spiritual giants, but they are not. Solomon,

who was a man with wisdom from God, gave a very interesting injunction: "Seest thou a man wise in his own conceit? there is more
hope of a fool than of him" (Prov. 26:12). I wouldn't dare say a thing
like this, but Solomon said it.

RELATIONSHIP TO UNBELIEVERS

You and I live in a world of unbelievers. What is to be our relationship with them?

> **Recompense to no man evil for evil. Provide things hon-
> est in the sight of all men.**
>
> **If it be possible, as much as lieth in you, live peaceably
> with all men [Rom. 12:17-18].**

"Recompense to no man evil for evil." The suggestion is that the believer may expect evil at the hands of the world. However, we are not
to strike back.

"Provide things honest in the sight of all men." There is nothing
that can hurt the cause of Christ more than a dishonest Christian. The
non-Christian is not concerned about the doctrine you hold—
whether you are a premillennialist or whether you believe in election
or free will. However, he does want to know if you are truthful or not,
and he does want to know if you pay your honest debts. Are you a
person that a man can depend upon? Providing things honest in the
sight of all men is a lot better than giving out tracts, my friend. Let me
illustrate this. Some years ago in Memphis, Tennessee, a Christian
handed a man a tract. "What is this?" asked the man. The Christian
replied, "It is a tract and I want you to read it." "I don't read," the man
replied, "but I will tell you what I will do—I will watch your tracks!"
Oh, how accurate that is! The world is watching the tracks that you
make, not the tracts you give out. Don't misunderstand me; giving out
gospel tracts is important. But you had better have a life that will back
them up when you give out tracts.

"If it be possible, as much as lieth in you, live peaceably"—I love this because there are people that you just cannot get along with; they won't let you get along with them. A dear lady who lived alone, a wonderful Christian, called me one day in deep concern because she had a neighbor whom she couldn't get along with, and she wondered if I would come and talk with the neighbor. As I was driving out there, I was thinking that since this lady had been living alone, although she was a Christian, she might be a little difficult herself. So I went out and talked to her neighbor. Well, the neighbor told me what she thought of me as well as this dear lady. I went back to this wonderful Christian and said, "I don't think you need to worry anymore if you can't get along with her. Nobody can get along with that woman. The Bible says 'as much as lieth in you'; it doesn't say you *have* to get along with her. Just do the best you can."

> **Dearly beloved, avenge not yourselves, but rather give place unto wrath: for it is written, Vengeance is mine; I will repay, saith the Lord.**

> **Therefore if thine enemy hunger, feed him; if he thirst, give him drink: for in so doing thou shalt heap coals of fire on his head [Rom. 12:19–20].**

This is one of the greatest principles you will find in the Word of God, yet it is the most difficult thing for a child of God to do. When somebody hits you on one cheek, it is difficult to turn the other cheek. I am like the Irishman who was hit on one cheek, and he got up and turned the other cheek. This time the fellow hit him so hard, he knocked him down. Then the Irishman got up and beat the stuffings out of the other fellow. Somebody asked him, "Why in the world did you do that? You turned the other cheek; why didn't you leave it like that?" "Well," he said, "the Bible says to turn your cheek, and I had only one other cheek to turn. The Lord didn't tell me what to do after that, so I did what I thought I ought to do." That is what most of us do. We find it difficult not to hit back. But the minute you and I take the matter into our own hands and attempt to work the thing out by hitting back as hard as we can, we have taken the matter out of God's control, and we are no longer walking by faith. God is saying to us, "You walk by faith with Me, and let Me handle the matter for you, because I will handle it in a just manner. If this person has injured you, I'll take care of him." You and I can turn these matters over to the Lord, and we ought to do that. I can tell you what to do, but I confess that I find it most difficult to do myself. But there have been one or two times when I have turned it over to the Lord, and I have been amazed at how well He handled it. He does it a lot better than I do it.

There was a man, an officer in one of the churches I served, who did me a great injury, a terrible injury. My first thought was to clobber him, but I remembered this passage of Scripture. I went to the Lord and said, "Lord, I'd like to hit back and I can, but I don't think I will. I'll turn him over to You, and I expect you to handle him." Well, I saw that man the other day. I have never looked at a person who is as unhappy as that man is. He has *troubles*, friend. The Lord has taken him to the woodshed and whipped him within an inch of his life. When I looked into that man's face, I couldn't help but feel sorry for him. I wish I could say that I turn all of these matters over to the Lord, but I confess that sometimes I hit back.

Be not overcome of evil, but overcome evil with good [Rom. 12:21].

In other words, stop being overcome of evil; overcome evil by means of good. As the believer walks through this evil world with its satanic system, he cannot fight it. If you attempt to fight this satanic system, my friend, it will whip you. You cannot adopt the same worldly tactics of hate and revenge. If you do, you can be assured of defeat.

"Overcome evil with good." God has given the believer the "good," which is the Holy Spirit. He is to walk in the Spirit. "This I say then, Walk in the Spirit, and ye shall not fulfill the lust of the flesh" (Gal. 5:16). Paul goes on to say, "If we live in the Spirit, let us also walk in the Spirit" (Gal. 5:25).

CHAPTER 13

THEME: Relationship to government; relationship to neighbors

As we come to chapter 13, we still are talking about the service of the sons of God. We are going to see that the believer has citizenship in heaven, but he also is a citizen in the world down here, which gives him a twofold responsibility. If there is a conflict between the two always our first responsibility is to our Lord in heaven.

The Lord Jesus made it very clear that we have a responsibility to human government. You remember that He was asked by His enemies, "Is it lawful to pay tribute to Caesar, or not?" He asked them to show Him a coin—He wanted to teach them from something they themselves had, and also I don't think He had a coin in His pocket that day. He didn't have much while He was down here in this world. He asked them whose superscription and whose image was on that coin. They said, "Ceasar's." Then He made this significant statement, ". . . Render therefore unto Caesar the things which be Caesar's, and unto God the things which be God's" (Luke 20:25).

Governments are ordained of God, and He gave them certain authority. At the very beginning of human government He said, "Whoso sheddeth man's blood, by man shall his blood be shed: for in the image of God made he man" (Gen. 9:6). God has a regard for human life; it is precious in His sight. You have no right to take another human life. If you do, you are to forfeit your own life. Our contemporary society feels differently about it and makes the criminal the hero and the honest man the villain. We live in a day when evil is called good and good is called evil. However, believers have a responsibility to human government. In fact, Paul said to a young preacher, "I exhort therefore, that, first of all, supplications, prayers, intercessions, and giving of thanks, be made for all men; For kings, and for all that are in authority; that we may lead a quiet and peaceable life in all godliness and honesty. For this is good and acceptable in the sight of God our

Saviour" (1 Tim. 2:1–3). By the way, we are to pray for those in authority, not leave it to the preacher on Sunday morning.

The duty of the believer as a citizen of heaven is spiritual. The duty of a believer as a citizen under a government is secular. These two are separate functions, and to combine them is to fail to keep church and state separate and distinct.

The Jew in Paul's day was reluctant to bow before the proud Roman state. Jewry had fomented disturbances in the city of Rome, and as a result Claudius had banished them on one occasion. The proud Pharisees rejected the Roman authorities in Palestine in their desire to restore the government to the nation of Israel; it was they who masterminded the encounter with Jesus and raised the issue, "Is it lawful to give tribute unto Caesar, or not?" The implications smacked of revolution, as you can see. It is well to remember that the authorities in Paul's day were mad and murderous. Nero was on the throne of Rome, and there was Pilate and Herod—all a bunch of rascals, yet he said that believers were to obey those in authority.

RELATIONSHIP TO GOVERNMENT

Let every soul be subject unto the higher powers. For there is no power but of God: the powers that be are ordained of God [Rom. 13:1].

We are to submit ourselves to governmental authorities for the very simple reason that they are ordained of God. It is true that the kingdoms of this world belong to Satan and that injustice and corruption abound in all governments; yet God still has control. History is the monotonous account of how a government flourished for a time in pomp and pride and then was brought to ruin and rubble. Why? Because corruption and lawlessness became rampant. As it did, God brought the government to an end. God still rules—even over this earth. God has not abdicated His throne; He is riding triumphantly in His own chariot. Neither is He disturbed about what is happening on this earth.

You will recall that when Uzziah, king of Judah, died, Isaiah was disturbed and very much discouraged. Uzziah had been a good king, and Isaiah thought the government would disintegrate after he was gone. So Isaiah went into the temple, which is a good place to go at a time like that. He came into God's presence, and He saw the Lord sitting upon the throne, high and lifted up. In other words, God had not abdicated. Uzziah was dead, but God was not dead. God was still on the throne.

Now the allegiance of the Christian is to *that* throne. And his relationship to his government on earth is submission.

> **Whosoever therefore resisteth the power, resisteth the ordinance of God: and they that resist shall receive to themselves damnation [Rom. 13:2].**

In other words, anyone resisting the authority is resisting the ordinance of God. And those resisting shall receive for themselves judgment.

The principle stated in verse 1 raised many questions which the following verses amplify and explain. This verse seems to preclude the possibility of a believer having any part in rebellion or revolution. What about it? James Stifler cites the examples of Cromwell and Washington. Both of those men led a revolution. Stifler offers no solution. I am not sure I have one either, but I am going to do the best I can to solve this. The believer has opposed bad government and supported good government on the theory that good government is the one ordained of God. The believer is for law and order, as over against lawlessness. He is for honesty and justice, as over against corruption and rank injustice. At great moments of crisis in history—and that's where we are today—the believers have had difficult decisions to make.

I want to briefly give you my viewpoint, and I believe that it will coincide with history. During these last days, which I believe we are in right now, lawlessness abounds. The believer must oppose it; he must not be a part of it, even when it is in his own government. We need to beware of those who would change our government under the guise of improving it. Remember John the Baptist was beheaded by Herod, Jesus was crucified under Pontius Pilate, James, the brother of

John, was slain with the sword of Herod, and Paul was put to death by
Nero. Yet Paul says, "Whosoever therefore resisteth the power, resisteth the ordinance of God: and they that resist shall receive to themselves damnation" (v. 2). Therefore, Christianity never became a
movement to improve government, help society, or clean up the town.
The gospel was the power of God unto salvation of the individual.
Paul never went around telling about the deplorable conditions of Roman jails—and he knew them well from the inside. When visiting
Rome, my wife and I went to the Mamertine prison, and I got claustro-
phobia down there. I said to my wife, "Let's get out of here!" But Paul
couldn't get out; they kept him down in that damp, dark prison. Remember he wrote to Timothy, "Bring my cloak with you" (see 2 Tim.
4:13)—he was getting cold down there.

It is very difficult to say that we are to obey a corrupt government. I
am not impressed by these men—preacher or politician—who are
running up the American flag and singing the national anthem as pro-
motion for themselves. And behind it is corruption. Frankly, I feel
resentful when I hear of certain government officials and certain
wealthy men in positions of power who pay no taxes at all when I have
a heavy tax burden. There is corruption in government from the top to
the bottom, and it is not confined to one party. These unsaved, godless men who are in positions of government actually do not understand the American system. You see, the men who made our laws had
a Bible background. I don't know that Thomas Jefferson was a
Christian—he was a deist—but he had great respect for the Word of
God. Many of those men were outstanding Christians—John Han-
cock, whose name is first on the Declaration of Independence, was a
real Christian. However, in our day the government is corrupt. I go to
the civic centers in our cities, and I see fine buildings, costing mil-
lions of dollars, which have been built by contractors who are friends
of the politicians. Also I see poverty areas. While both parties talk
about eliminating poverty, the poverty remains. Oh, corruption is
there. What's wrong? Well, the thing wrong is the human heart.

What is the Christian to do? My business is to get out the Word of
God, and my business is to obey the law. That is what Paul is saying
here. Christianity is not a movement to improve government or to help

society clean up the town. It is to preach a gospel that is the power of God unto salvation which will bring into existence individuals like the men who signed the Declaration of Independence and gave us a government of laws.

My friend, nothing is wrong with our form of government; there is something wrong with the individuals who are in positions of power. A professor in the history department of the University of Michigan summed it up well when he said, "America is in the hands of those who do not understand the spiritual heritage that we have."

> **For rulers are not a terror to good works, but to the evil. Wilt thou then not be afraid of the power? do that which is good, and thou shalt have praise of the same:**

> **For he is the minister of God to thee for good. But if thou do that which is evil, be afraid; for he beareth not the sword in vain: for he is the minister of God, a revenger to execute wrath upon him that doeth evil [Rom. 13:3–4].**

The government is to maintain law and order. When it does not do that, it has failed. I feel that a Christian should be opposed to the breakdown of law and order. We are to respect our rulers who are enforcing the law. I have great respect for our army, although it is honeycombed with corruption. I have great respect for police officers, although I know they make mistakes.

> **Wherefore ye must needs be subject, not only for wrath, but also for conscience sake [Rom. 13:5].**

Christians are to obey the law not only because we'll be judged and have to pay a fine if we don't, but obey for conscience sake.

> **For for this cause pay ye tribute also: for they are God's ministers, attending continually upon this very thing [Rom. 13:6].**

Although we may resent the way our tax money is being used, we are to pay taxes anyway.

In this verse the word for minister is one from which we get our word *liturgy*. It is strictly religious and is the same word used of angels in Hebrews 1:14 where they are called ministering spirits. This means that the ruler occupies a divinely-appointed office. He has no religious function, of course, but he holds a God-appointed office. That makes me pay my taxes, although I resent doing so.

We need today a heaven-sent revival. I am sick and tired of those who are shedding crocodile tears. They remind me of Lewis Carroll's brilliant satire, *Alice in Wonderland*. You remember that the Walrus and the Carpenter in this story were walking along the seashore weeping because there was so much sand and not enough oysters. They kept on eating and eating and weeping and weeping. What a picture of corruption! But in all of this the believer should submit to his government.

> **Render therefore to all their dues: tribute to whom tribute is due; custom to whom custom; fear to whom fear; honour to whom honour [Rom. 13:7].**

Although there may be unworthy men in the office, we are to respect the office. When I was in the army, I was told to salute the uniform. There were some folk in that uniform that I didn't care about saluting, but I saluted the uniform. We are to show respect for authority. A Christian will be the best citizen although his citizenship is in heaven.

RELATIONSHIP TO NEIGHBORS

> **Owe no man any thing, but to love one another: for he that loveth another hath fulfilled the law [Rom. 13:8].**

Did you borrow your neighbor's lawnmower? Take it back to him. Housewife, did you borrow a cup of sugar from your neighbor? Return it, please. Owe no one anything, In this we find Paul saying that the believer is positively to owe no man anything but love. This is a great principle to guide Christians in installment purchasing. You may ask, "Do you think we should turn in our credit cards?" No, but you had better be able to see your way clear in order to pay your debts.

The believer always owes the debt of love to his neighbor. That does not necessarily mean the man next door, but all people with whom you come in contact. This love is not some sentimental thing. I get a little disturbed when I hear liberalism continually talk about love, love, love. How do you reveal love?

> **For this, Thou shalt not commit adultery, Thou shalt not kill, Thou shalt not steal, Thou shalt not bear false witness, Thou shalt not covet; and if there be any other commandment, it is briefly comprehended in this saying, namely, Thou shalt love thy neighbor as thyself [Rom. 13:9].**

"Thou shalt not commit adultery." Now don't tell me that you love someone and are committing adultery with that one. You can call that love if you want to, but it is nothing in the world but sex. It is licentiousness, it is fornication, and it is sin in God's sight. God hasn't changed His mind about it.

"Thou shalt not kill." You can kill a person in more ways than pulling a trigger of a gun. You can destroy them by ruining their reputation.

"Thou shalt not steal." If you love, you won't get something dishonestly.

"Thou shalt not covet." When your neighbor drives up in a new automobile, how do you feel about it? Sometimes we say, "I wish we had the car and they had one just like it." What we really mean is that we would rather have that car than see them have it.

Paul is saying that our love for our neighbor is revealed in what we do rather than in what we say. He is not putting the Christian back under the Law; he is saying that love manifests itself in not committing adultery, not killing, not stealing, not coveting. You can talk about love all you want to, but if you commit these acts against your neighbor, you have no love for him.

Love worketh no ill to his neighbour: therefore love is the fulfilling of the law [Rom. 13:10].

Loving your neighbor is the fullness of the Law. This love, let me repeat, is the fruit of the Spirit.

And that, knowing the time, that now it is high time to awake out of sleep: for now is our salvation nearer than when we believed.

The night is far spent, the day is at hand: let us therefore cast off the works of darkness, and let us put on the armour of light [Rom. 13:11–12].

Paul said this nineteen hundred years ago, and certainly we ought to say it with a little more urgency in this day in which we are living. Let me give you my translation: And this—seeing that ye know the time or the season, that now it is the hour for you to wake out of sleep, for now is our salvation nearer than when we believed. The night is passing, it is far spent, and the day is at hand; let us therefore cast off the works of darkness, and let us put on the armor of light.

In this closing section an alarm clock goes off to waken believers who have gone to sleep in the world and have forgotten this added incentive for yielding their total personalities to God. My friend, this is not the time for the child of God to live for the things of this world. I think many a rich Christian is going to be embarrassed when the Lord comes. How big will your bank account be, my friend? Are you using your time and what you possess for God? I beseech you therefore, brethren, by the mercies of God, that ye yield your total personalities—all you are, all you have—to God. This is rational. This is reasonable. This is what you are supposed to be doing, Christian friend.

If we really are looking for the return of Christ, it will purify our lives. "And every man that hath this hope in him purifieth himself, even as he is pure" (1 John 3:3). These fellows who get divorces and live like the world, then talk about being premillennial and pretribulational and looking for the imminent coming of Christ, are not being honest. The apostle John says that that man is a liar! Let us wake up, my friend. Let us live for *God* in this hour!

> **Let us walk honestly, as in the day; not in rioting and drunkenness, not in chambering and wantonness, not in strife and envying [Rom. 13:13].**

In other words, let us walk honorably as those in the day; not in revelings and drunkenness, not in sexual intercourse and dissolute abandon, not in strife and jealousy.

We hear a great deal about night life. The believer is identified with day life. He walks as one who belongs to the day.

> **But put ye on the Lord Jesus Christ, and make not provision for the flesh, to fulfil the lusts thereof [Rom. 13:14].**

Oh, how many believers are making every provision for the flesh but are making no provision to go into His presence. My friend, I beg you to put Christ first in your life and to get out the Word of God. This is all-important.

CHAPTER 14

THEME: Conviction; conscience

This chapter brings us to a new section, the final division in the Epistle to the Romans. It is: the separation of the "sons of God." What do we mean by separation? Frankly, I am tired of "separated" and "dedicated" Christians who are not separated or really dedicated.

There are two areas of Christian conduct. In one area the Bible is very clear, as we saw in the preceding chapter. The duty of the Christian to the state is submission. He is to obey the laws of the land, he is to pay his taxes, and he is to show respect to those in authority. Also chapter 13 was specific on a believer's relationship to his neighbor. He is to pay his bills; he is not to commit adultery, kill, steal, bear false witness, or covet what another has. In fact, he is to love his neighbor as himself. The believer is to be honest, and he is to avoid reveling and drunkenness, strife, and jealousy. The Bible is very clear on these things.

However, there is another area of Christian conduct on which the Bible has no clear word. Let me mention only two things: the use of tobacco and mixed bathing (that is, both sexes swimming together). If you don't think these are questionable, let me give you an illustration out of my own experience. My wife was reared in Texas in a Southern Baptist church. She was brought up by a mother and father and pastor who believed that mixed bathing was sinful. Then when she came to California, you can't imagine the shock she had the first time she went down to the beach with the young people from our church—even in those days they weren't wearing much. My wife was in a state of shock for twenty-four hours after that! She had never seen anything like it. However, in the area from which she came the use of tobacco was not frowned upon. The officers of her church smoked; in fact, her pastor smoked. When she came to California, she found that using tobacco was taboo. If you were a Christian, you did not smoke.

Is mixed bathing all right in one place and wrong in another place?

Is smoking right in one place and wrong in another place? I am sure that the hair on the back of the necks of some of the saints is standing on end, and they are thinking, *Dr. McGee, you ought to give a lecture against smoking, and you let this subject of mixed bathing alone.* Let me assure you that I am not condemning either one, not am I condoning either one. I'm not going to stick out my neck on questionable things any farther than Paul stuck out his neck.

In this section Paul puts down principles of conduct for Christians relative to questionable matters. He gives us three guidelines: conviction, conscience, and consideration. A Christian should have a conviction about what he does. *Conviction* means "that which anticipates." Does he look forward to what he is going to do in high anticipation and enthusiasm? The second guideline is conscience. Does he look back on what he has done, wondering if he were right or wrong? Or does he even hate himself for what he has done? The third guideline is consideration for others. Are other people adversely affected by what he does? These three guidelines give us principles of conduct for our Christian lives.

In our day there are actually two extreme viewpoints about this matter of Christian conduct in questionable matters. And it has created an artificial atmosphere in which one is to live the Christian life. As a result we have abnormal or subnormal Christians in these extreme areas. One extreme position has no wall of separation from the world; the lives of these folk are carbon copies of the unsaved man of the world. Their lives are no different from what they were before their so-called conversion. They indulge in all forms of worldly amusement. They go everywhere the world goes, and they spend their time and energy in activities that have no spiritual profit. There are certain passages of Scripture that have no meaning for them at all. For example: "Brethren, be followers together of me, and mark them which walk so as ye have us for an ensample. (For many walk, of whom I have told you often, and now tell you even weeping, that they are the enemies of the cross of Christ: Whose end is destruction, whose God is their belly, and whose glory is in their shame, who mind earthly things.)" (Phil. 3:17–19). There are other folk who do not indulge in any form of worldly amusement, yet they are as worldly as they can possibly be. They gorge and gormandize themselves. They don't get drunk, but they certainly overeat. Also they overtalk—they are great gossips. They even tell questionable stories.

Again let me quote Paul: "Finally, brethren, whatsoever things are true, whatsoever things are honest, whatsoever things are just, whatsoever things are pure, whatsoever things are lovely, whatsoever things are of good report; if there be any virtue, and if there be any praise, think on these things" (Phil. 4:8). My friend, your thought life is bound to affect your conduct sooner of later. What you keep thinking about you will eventually do. I have found that a great many Christians think about a temptation for a long time before they actually submit to it. This sort of thing is done by a great many so-called Christians. Paul seemed to question whether or not they were Christians because they lived exactly as the worldling lived.

Now there is a second group that is extreme in the opposite direction. They have reduced the Christian life to a series of negatives. Paul warned the Colossian believers against the group that was characterized by "Touch not; taste not; handle not" (Col. 2:21). These folk rejoice in salvation by grace and deliverance from the Mosaic Law, but they immediately make a new set of ten commandments—only they usually double that number. They become very self-centered, very critical, and very proud. These are the ones that Paul labels "weak in the faith" (v. 1), by the way. And they are the folk who have become very "separated."

The following letter which I received several years ago illustrates the sad state of one who adopts this position.

I've returned to California after a year of full-time Christian service in Ohio and an extended trip east. But I've come back almost spiritually shipwrecked! Have been a Christian for three and one-half years and until recently was able to give a glowing testimony about being saved out of Unity.

But lately, I've been so dead that Christ seems way up there, and I'm way down here. I have all the negative virtues of a Christian (don't smoke, drink, play cards, attend movies, use makeup), but those things do not make a happy Christian! My

friends tell me I'm becoming bitter—and oh, I don't want that
to happen!

Before becoming a Christian, I was very ambitious, worked
hard for whatever I believed in (and incidently I was listed in
Who's Who)—but now I wonder what's the use? The world is
going from bad to worse. Everything is heading for disaster,
and the only hope is to wait for the return of the Lord Jesus
Christ.

Now, my friend, this person was in a terrible condition! Notice how
"separated" she was, but this kind of separation will not bring joy in
the life.

Somewhere between these two extreme viewpoints of questionable matters in Christian conduct the believer is to walk. These are the
Scylla and Charybdis through which the believer must sail his little
bark on the sea of life.

I have given a great deal of space to these preliminary remarks
because I know there are many puzzled Christians who will be helped
by what Paul has for us in this important chapter.

> **Him that is weak in the faith receive ye, but not to doubt-
> ful disputations [Rom. 14:1].**

To put it another way: Now, the one who is weak in faith, receive him
into your fellowship, but not with the view of passing judgment upon
his scruples—that is, upon his conduct and upon his viewpoint.

"Now" connects this chapter to what has preceded it. The law of
love will now go into action. Having condemned things (in the last
part of Romans 13) which are immoral and obviously wrong, like killing, committing adultery, stealing, bearing false witness, and coveting, Paul now warns against the danger of condemning questionable
matters which are not expressly forbidden in Scripture.

"The one who is weak in the faith" does not mean one who is weak
in the great truths of the gospel—the facts of faith—but rather it refers
to the abstract quality of faith. It means the faith of the weak falters
and hesitates about matters of conduct. He does not know what he

should do relative to certain things. This one is to be received into the fellowship of believers with open arms. You may not agree with him, but you are to receive him if he is a believer in Jesus Christ. You are not to receive him in order to start an argument about questionable things. One group of believers is not to sit in judgment upon another group of believers about questionable matters of Christian conduct. Some things are not expressly condemned in Scripture, but some believers separate themselves from these things. And if they want to do this, that's their business. These things are not to separate believers. *The Scofield Reference Bible* has a very helpful note on this verse— "The church has no authority to decide questions of personal liberty in things not expressly forbidden in Scripture."

For one believeth that he may eat all things: another, who is weak, eateth herbs [Rom. 14:2].

This verse may hurt the extreme separationist. The *strong* brother in the faith is the one eating all things; the *weak* brother is the vegetarian. The strong brother realizes that Jesus made all meats clean, "cleansing all meats" (see Mark 7:19). After the Flood God gave all meats to be eaten according to Genesis 9:3, "Every moving thing that liveth shall be meat for you; even as the green herb have I given you all things."

God made a distinction between clean and unclean animals for the nation Israel. The instructed believer knows this does not apply to him, for the apostle says in 1 Corinthians 8:8, "But meat commendeth us not to God: for neither, if we eat, are we the better; neither, if we eat not, are we the worse." You remember that Peter was given a practical lesson about this subject on the housetop of Simon the tanner in Joppa (see Acts 10:9–16). Peter was proud of the fact that he had not eaten anything unclean. Boy, was he separated, and he was proud of it! The Holy Spirit said to him, ". . . What God hath cleansed, that call not thou common" (Acts 10:15).

Paul could eat meat without his conscience bothering him, but Peter had scruples about it. The weak believer who has a background of eating vegetables finds eating meat repugnant to him.

What is the principle? One can eat meat and the other cannot eat meat. By the grace of God one is not to eat meat and the other is to eat meat. Now listen to Paul:

Let not him that eateth despise him that eateth not; and let not him which eateth not judge him that eateth: for God hath received him [Rom. 14:3].

I recognize that I am wrong when I condemn these extreme separationists. If they want to be that way, candidly, that is their business. The thing that upsets me is that they want to straighten me out. I know I need straightening out, but they are not the crowd to do it, I'm sure of that. One group is not to condemn the other. If you believe that you should not eat meat (he uses meat as an example, but this could apply to anything else not expressly forbidden in Scripture), then you should not eat meat, my friend. But if you believe that you can eat meat, then you go ahead and eat meat.

Who art thou that judgest another man's servant? to his own master he standeth or falleth. Yea, he shall be holden up: for God is able to make him stand [Rom. 14:4].

This is devastating. Paul asks, "What right have you to judge another man's servant?" What right have you, Christian friend, to sit in judgment on another Christian's conduct when it involves something that is questionable? Are you God? Is that person accountable to you? Paul says, "He is not accountable to you. He is accountable to God. He is going to stand before his own Master."

Can you imagine being a dinner guest in someone's home, and the servant brings in cold biscuits. You say to the servant, "What's the big idea of bringing me cold biscuits?" And you chide—in our common colloquialism, *bawl out*—the servant! May I say to you, there would be an awkward silence in that home. That person is not your servant. Maybe she should not have served cold biscuits, but it is not your place to say so. I have a notion that the lady of the house will go back to the kitchen and will tend to the matter.

Now maybe you disapprove of my conduct in one of these doubtful areas. I don't have to account to you; you are not my master. I am responsible to Jesus Christ. He is my Master.

CONVICTION

Paul gives us now the first great principle of conduct for Christians:

> **One man esteemeth one day above another: another esteemeth every day alike. Let every man be fully persuaded in his own mind [Rom. 14:5].**

"Fully persuaded" means to be convinced, to be assured in your own mind.

Now Paul changes his illustration from diet to the *day* question. Some people insist that the Lord's Day is different. Some observe Sunday as the Lord's Day and others observe Saturday. It is not the *day* that should be different, but the *believer*. The particular day is not the important thing. Paul said, "Let no man therefore judge you in meat, or in drink, or in respect of an holyday, or of the new moon, or of the sabbath days" (Col. 2:16). Don't you tell me what day I am to observe. I'm not responsible to you; I am responsible to the Lord Jesus. He is my Master.

When I was a student in seminary, I was in a denomination in the South that were strict Sabbatarians—Sunday was their Sabbath, as they called it. And they didn't believe in traveling on Sunday. I used to take a train to Augusta, Georgia, to preach, and I left on Saturday evening. Some of the officers of the church wanted to know what time the train got into Augusta! Well, it got in early Sunday morning, and one man said to me, "Doesn't that disturb you?" I said, "It doesn't disturb me at all." Now, I respect that man, and I don't think he ought to travel on Sunday. But when I am traveling from one speaking engagement to another, and it is necessary to travel on Sunday, I do it without the slightest compunction. Paul says that whatever we do, we should be fully persuaded, convinced, and assured in our own mind that it is the right thing to do.

"Let every man be fully persuaded in his own mind" means literally he is to be filled to the brim—mind, heart, will, and the total personality. A believer should do only those things to which he can give himself fully and without reserve. My friend, whatever you do for God, you should do with enthusiasm. I think it is sinful the way some people go to church on Sunday. Can you imagine people going to a football game when the alma mater is playing with that same lackluster attitude they have when they attend church? Personally, I don't go to football games because I think they are a waste of time. But I don't criticize other folk for going—that's their business. But when I go to play golf, I go with enthusiasm. And whatever I do for the Lord, I do with enthusiasm. I teach the Bible because I love to teach it. I would rather do it than anything I know of. One of the reasons church work is bogged down as it is today is that there is a lack of enthusiasm. A man is asked to teach a Sunday school class, and he says, "Oh, if you can't get anybody else, I'll take it." Then don't take it, brother, if that is the way you feel. It would be better for the class to have no teacher than a disinterested, unenthusiastic teacher. Some people are actually committing sin by doing church work! The first great principle is: "Let every man be fully persuaded in his own mind."

Now let's bring this principle over to questionable things. Frequently folk, especially young folk, ask me if doing this or that is wrong. I say, "Well, for you I think it is wrong, but for me it's all right." Of course they ask me what I mean by that. I tell them, "I have no question about it. If I wanted to do it, I would do it with enthusiasm. The point is, you have a question about it. 'Let every man be fully persuaded in his own mind.' You wouldn't have come and asked me the question if you had been persuaded in your own mind." My friend, this is a great guiding principle: if you have a question in your mind about something you are doing—whatever it is—for you it is wrong. It might not be wrong for me, but it is certainly wrong for you.

You recall that Simon Peter followed the Lord afar off after He was arrested. Peter went that night into the judgment hall of the high priest. I sat in the hotel in Jerusalem in the old city on the side of the Valley of Kidron one morning. When the morning sun had come up, it set that whole city ablaze across the Kidron Valley. Over there is a church called the Church of the Cock Crowing. It is situated on the spot where the high priest's judgment hall was located—that's where Caiaphas had his home. And that is the place to which Simon Peter came and where he denied three times that he knew the Lord. I am convinced that Simon Peter should not have gone there that night. On the other hand, John, who apparently had a home in Jerusalem and was known in the palace of the high priest, went there and did not deny his Lord. It was all right for John to be there, but it was wrong for Simon Peter. Simon Peter was the weak brother, you see.

Today it is the weak brother who is the "separated" brother. That may seem strange to you. But the people who set up a little legal system of "dos" and "don'ts" bear watching. They are the weak ones. When I was a student in seminary, I used to have a water fight on Saturday night in the seminary dorm. One of the students would gather together two or three of the super-duper saints, and they would pray for us. (I always hoped he would pray that I would win!) We were pretty rough fellows. One night we soaked all the rugs, and we almost got booted out of the place. But this young fellow was a model student. About fifteen years later, I sat down with him and his wife and begged him not to leave her. He told me he had to. I said, "Why?" His reply was this, "Because I have a little daughter by a woman out in Australia, and I want to marry her." He posed as a super-duper saint, but actually he was a weak brother.

Questionable amusements are wrong for the believer if they are questionable to him. If he can participate in them and maintain a close relationship to Christ, they are not wrong for him. Let me tell you a little story in this connection. Many years ago in Tennessee a young lady went to her pastor with the question, "Do you think it is wrong for a Christian to dance?" He said to her, "Anywhere you can take Jesus Christ with you is all right to go." That made her angry. She said, "Well, I can take Him to the dance." The pastor said, "Then go ahead." So she went to the dance. A boy whom she had not met before cut in on her and danced with her. She had determined to take Jesus

Christ with her, so she asked him, "Are you a Christian?" He said, "No." Wanting to make conversation with her, he asked, "Are you a Christian?" She said, "Yes." And this is what the unbeliever said, "Then what are you doing here?" After she got home that night she decided that maybe she couldn't take the Lord Jesus Christ there after all.

> He that regardeth the day, regardeth it unto the Lord; and he that regardeth not the day, to the Lord he doth not regard it. He that eateth, eateth to the Lord, for he giveth God thanks; and he that eateth not, to the Lord he eateth not, and giveth God thanks [Rom. 14:6].

Maybe you play golf on Sunday. If you can take Jesus Christ with you, if you can stop out on the ninth hole and have a prayer meeting with the foursome you are playing with, that would be fine. But what will the foursome playing behind you think when their game is interrupted in this way? When they see you are praying, one of them will say, "What in the world are they doing out here on Sunday morning?"

The important thing to note is that the day is to be "regarded" or observed unto the Lord.

Also, the one who eats meat gives thanks to God from his heart. The one who does not eat meat gives thanks to God from his heart. It is not what is on the table, but what is in the heart that is noted by God. It is the heart attitude that conditions Christian conduct.

> For none of us liveth to himself, and no man dieth to himself.

> For whether we live, we live unto the Lord; and whether we die, we die unto the Lord: whether we live therefore, or die, we are the Lord's.

> For to this end Christ both died, and rose, and revived, that he might be Lord both of the dead and living [Rom. 14:7–9].

"None of us liveth to himself, and no man dieth to himself" is generally quoted as a proof text that our lives affect others. However, that thought is not in this passage. The fact is that we as Christians cannot live our lives apart from Christ. Whether you live, you will have to live to Him; whether you die, you will have to die to Him. Our Christian conduct is not gauged by the foods spread out on the table, but by the fact that our lives are spread out before Him. That is the important thing. One day we are going to have to give an account of the things we have done in this life. "For we must all appear before the judgment seat of Christ; that every one may receive the things done in his body, according to that he hath done, whether it be good or bad" (2 Cor. 5:10). At that time it will not be a question of the meat you had on the table; it will be the question of your relationship to Him when you sat down at that table. You can be godless without meat; and you can be godless with meat, of course.

Christ's death and resurrection are given as grounds for Him to exercise lordship over both the dead and the living:

> **But why dost thou judge thy brother? or why dost thou set at nought thy brother? for we shall all stand before the judgment seat of Christ.**
>
> **For it is written, As I live, saith the Lord, every knee shall bow to me, and every tongue shall confess to God.**
>
> **So then every one of us shall give account of himself to God [Rom. 14:10–12].**

"Why dost thou judge thy brother?" You remember that the Lord Jesus said to that bunch of Pharisees who wanted to stone an adulterous woman, ". . . He that is without sin among you, let him first cast a stone at her" (John 8:7). And not one of those boys threw any stones that day. My friend, you and I need to recognize that we have to give account of *ourselves* to Him. I'll be honest with you, that disturbs me a little. I am wondering how I am going to tell Him about certain things. So I can't sit in judgment upon you; I'm worried about Vernon McGee.

> Let us not therefore judge one another any more: but
> judge this rather, that no man put a stumblingblock or
> an occasion to fall in his brother's way [Rom. 14:13].

Paul is going to develop the thought that our conduct has to be for the
sake of the weak brother. If I am traveling in the same car with a fellow
who believes he should not travel on Sunday, I'm going to have to stay
with him—not because I agree with him, but for the sake of a weak
brother.

> I know, and am persuaded by the Lord Jesus, that there
> is nothing unclean of itself: but to him that esteemeth
> any thing to be unclean, to him it is unclean.
>
> But if thy brother be grieved with thy meat, now walkest
> thou not charitably. Destroy not him with thy meat, for
> whom Christ died [Rom. 14:14–15].

Since Christ was willing to die for that weak brother, certainly we
ought to be willing to refrain from eating something or doing something that would hurt him in his Christian walk.

> Let not then your good be evil spoken of [Rom. 14:16].

In other words, liberty does not mean license. The believer is to use
his liberty, not *abuse* it. We are always to keep in mind how our conduct will affect weaker Christians.

> For the kingdom of God is not meat and drink; but righ-
> teousness, and peace, and joy in the Holy Ghost [Rom.
> 14:17].

This is the only reference in this epistle to the Kingdom of God. I do
not believe the "kingdom of God" is synonymous with the Kingdom
of Heaven in Matthew's Gospel, which finds its final fruition in the
millennial and messianic Kingdom here on earth. I believe that the

Kingdom of God embraces all that is in God's created universe, which, of course, includes the church. It is broader and larger and includes God's reign over all His creation. Lange's definition is satisfactory: "The heavenly sphere of life in which God's word and Spirit govern, and whose organ on earth is the Church." This was our Lord's use of the term. "Jesus answered and said unto him, Verily, verily, I say unto thee, Except a man be born again, he cannot see the kingdom of God" (John 3:3). Well, that is the heavenly sphere of life in which God's Word and Spirit govern. As Stifler has said (*The Epistle to the Romans*, p. 245), "God rules everywhere, but there is a realm where he governs by spiritual forces or laws alone"—which is in the area of the life of the believer. Man is totally incapable of seeing or entering this kingdom without the new birth. This kingdom has nothing to do with eating or drinking, fasting, no meat on Friday, no pork, or a vegetarian diet. These things just do not enter into it.

"Righteousness'" in this verse means the same as it does in chapters 1 and 3. It means to be right with God; it means a life lived well-pleasing to Him.

"Holy Ghost" apparently goes with righteousness and refers, not to our standing, but to our walk—we are to walk in the Spirit. It is practical rather than theological. It is moral rather than oral. It is a righteousness in the Holy Spirit rather than righteousness in Christ.

"Joy" is the fruit of the Holy Spirit in the lives of believers. Unfortunately, it is often absent from the lives of believers. There should be joy in our lives. This doesn't mean you have to run around smiling like a Cheshire cat, but it does mean you are to have a joyful feeling deep in your heart.

> **For he that in these things serveth Christ is acceptable to God, and approved of men [Rom. 14:18].**

Although, of course, there will be a literal kingdom on this earth, he is talking here about the spiritual realm that you enter by the new birth. Christ is not served by eating and drinking, but our service to Him must pertain to righteousness, peace, and joy in the Holy Spirit. In these things a believer is well-pleasing to God and approved of men.

"Approved of men" does not mean that men will get in your cheering section and applaud you because you are a believer. They may even persecute you. But underneath, men do approve of genuine believers, while they despise and reject that which is hypocritical and phony.

This is a great principle of conduct. The walk and talk of the believer should please God and meet the approval of the conscience of men.

> **Let us therefore follow after the things which make for peace, and things wherewith one may edify another [Rom. 14:19].**

This is a twofold exhortation. To "follow after the things which make for peace" is to eagerly pursue this course of action. The believer is to make a definite effort to avoid the use of food or any physical thing which offends a Christian brother. This would be the negative aspect of the exhortation. The positive aspect is to press toward the mark of spiritual values: righteousness, peace, and joy in the Holy Spirit. These are the things which build up the believer.

> **For meat destroy not the work of God. All things indeed are pure; but it is evil for that man who eateth with offence [Rom. 14:20].**

On account of food, do not tear down the work of God. Of course the believer has the liberty to eat meat or abstain from it—but neither will commend him to God. We are not to tear down the work of God in the heart of some weak believer for the sake of some physical gratification. That old bromide is active: one man's porridge is another man's poison. Esau, for instance, had no regard for God or for his birthright. He exchanged it for a bowl of soup. Well, don't sell your birthright just to satisfy your appetite.

> **It is good neither to eat flesh, nor to drink wine, nor any thing whereby thy brother stumbleth, or is offended, or is made weak [Rom. 14:21].**

Paul returns to these two points: eating and drinking. Then he goes beyond them with the sweeping statement: *nor anything*. Anything that is questionable and is a matter of conscience for a weak brother becomes wrong for the strong one.

CONSCIENCE

Now verse 22 gives us the second great principle of Christian conduct.

Hast thou faith? have it to thyself before God. Happy is he that condemneth not himself in that thing which he alloweth [Rom. 14:22].

Let me give you my translation of this verse; The faith which thou hast, have thou thyself in the sight of God. Happy is the man who condemneth not himself in the things which he approves—that which he does.

This is the second principle of conduct for Christians. He has already dealt with the aspect of conviction. As we look toward doing something for God, we ask ourselves the questions: Will it be right for me to do this? Can I do it with excitement and anticipation and joy? Now this second exhortation looks back at what has been done. Happy is the man who does not condemn himself in what he has done. The believer should be able to look back upon his conduct without any qualms of conscience.

Let me use an illustration, and I trust you will not misunderstand it. I have been asked the question: "Can a Christian get drunk?" The answer is yes. The prodigal son in Luke 15 was a son out in the far country. I am confident that he got drunk in addition to a few other things, but he was always a son. Then what was the difference between him and the pigs? The difference was that none of those pigs said, "I will arise and go to my father." You see, as the prodigal son was there with the pigs, he said to himself, *I hate it here, and I'm going to get out of this. I am going back to my father and confess what a sinner I am.* What, then, is the difference between the Christian who gets drunk and the non-Christian who gets drunk? The difference is simply this: the next morning the man of the world will get up with a headache, put an ice pack on it, and say, "Boy, I sure had a big time! I'm going to get a bigger bucket of paint and a bigger paint brush, and I am really going to paint the town red the next time!" But what will the child of God do? When he wakes up the next morning with a head as big as a barrel, he drops down by the side of his bed and cries, "Oh, God, I hate myself! I don't want to do that again." He confesses his sins to God. And the interesting thing is there is no record that the prodigal son went back to the pig pen. He didn't like it there. That is the difference between a believer and an unbeliever. "Happy is he that condemneth not himself in that thing which he alloweth."

My Christian friend, do you look back and hate yourself for what you have done? That is your conscience condemning you. Regardless of what it was and regardless of how many other people do the same thing, for you it was *wrong*. You might have been in a church (and a church can be a very dangerous place because Satan is there—he goes to church every Sunday morning, and he goes to the best churches). Do you come home from church and say, "I could bite my tongue off. I wish I hadn't said what I did." Well, you should not have said it. "Happy is he that condemneth not himself in that thing which he alloweth."

And he that doubteth is damned if he eat, because he eateth not of faith: for whatsoever is not of faith is sin [Rom. 14:23].

"Whatsoever is not of faith is sin." My friend, you are to believe in what you are doing. If you don't believe in it, you should not be doing it. Here is a new definition of sin for the believer: Any line of conduct or any act which is not the outflow of faith becomes sin. This is the Holy Spirit's answer of questionable things. As the believer is saved by faith, just so the believer is to walk by faith.

CHAPTER 15

THEME: Consideration of the weak brother; consolidation of Jews and Gentiles in one body; continuation of Paul's personal testimony

We have been looking at the great principles of conduct for the Christian. In the preceding chapter we have seen two of these principles: conviction and conscience. Now we see the third: consideration of the weak brother, a thought which is continued from chapter 14. In the first three verses the subject is separation. Then we shall see the consolidation of Jews and Gentiles in one body to glorify God, and finally the continuation of Paul's personal testimony as the apostle to the Gentiles and to the Romans in particular. This chapter concludes the major argument of the Epistle to the Romans. In the final chapter, Paul will lapse back to personal relationships.

A remark needs to be made here that radical higher criticism has questioned the authenticity of these last two chapters of Romans. Without any valid reason or documentary evidence, the Pauline authorship of these two chapters was rejected. Baur's school led in this objection. Today the Pauline authorship is established, and we may conclude with this statement from Kerr in his *Introduction to New Testament Study*, "Despite these objections, the integrity of the epistle as it now stands is certain."

CONSIDERATION OF THE WEAK BROTHER

We then that are strong ought to bear the infirmities of the weak, and not to please ourselves [Rom. 15:1].

This is the third and last guiding principle which should govern the conduct of Christians. When you invite a Christian over to your house who doesn't believe in dancing, don't put on a square dance for him, because you will offend him. Now maybe you can square dance, but I cannot. Why? Because there are certain things I very definitely feel I cannot do because of a consideration of others. Neither have I been inside a motion picture theater in years—I can't even remember the last time I went. Somebody says, "Oh, you are one of those separated fellows who doesn't believe you can go to the movies." Maybe you can go—I'm not judging you if you do—but I cannot. One of the reasons is right here: consideration of the weak brother. "We that are strong" I feel applies to me. I feel that I could go without losing my fellowship with the Lord—I'm sure that many of these movies would disgust me today, to tell the truth. But a weak brother might be strongly influenced and his relationship to Christ actually damaged by certain movies. So we who are strong ought to bear the infirmities of the weak.

Paul identifies himself with the strong ones, and he insists that these should show consideration for the feelings and prejudices of the weak believers. He wrote to the Corinthians, "Wherefore, if meat make my brother to offend, I will eat no flesh while the world standeth, lest I make my brother to offend" (1 Cor. 8:13). In other words, Paul said, "I can eat meat. I love a good pork roast. But I will not eat it if it is going to offend my brother." Also Paul wrote, "Let no man seek his own but every man another's wealth" (1 Cor. 10:24). Seek the interest of the other man. "Bear ye one another's burdens, and so fulfil the law of Christ" (Gal. 6:2).

Let every one of us please his neighbor for his good to edification [Rom. 15:2].

"For his good to edification" means with a view to his building up. The objective of all Christian conduct is the edification of our neighbor. Of course our neighbor is not to be pleased to his detriment or loss. Paul said, "For thou I be free from all men, yet have I made myself servant unto all, that I might gain the more. And unto the Jews I became as a Jew, that I might gain the Jews . . ." (1 Cor. 9:19–20). A great many people criticize Paul and cannot understand why he would take a Jewish oath, shave his head, and go to Jerusalem to the temple. You will understand it if you understand what Paul is saying

Infirmities are the shortcoming of the weak
Love must be rough & strong

Christian fellowship study of scripture
3 Hope produces 4 Wisdom
3 Harmony 5 praise

here: "And unto the Jews I became as a Jew, that I might gain the Jews; to them that are under the law, as under the law, that I might gain them that are under the law" (1 Cor. 9:20).

Now let's keep in mind that we are still in the area of questionable things, things that are not mentioned in Scripture as wrong. Going back to the example of the movies. Would I ever go to a movie? Yes, if I thought by so doing I could win someone for Christ. You may ask, "How far can you carry this?" Well, I know a group that went into a burlesque show to witness. I think they were in the wrong place. I know a girl who started going to nightclubs and drinking with her friends, thinking she could witness to them. But she became an alcoholic, and she didn't win anybody. I can show you from Scripture that these things are wrong.

However, because the Scripture is silent on many things in our contemporary society, we have been given these great guidelines, three principles of separation: (1) Conviction. Whatever we do is to be done with enthusiasm because we are persuaded in our own minds that it is what God wants us to do. (2) Conscience. Our conduct should be such that we do not look back upon it with qualms of conscience. (3) Consideration. We should show consideration for the feelings and prejudices of the weak believers.

1 Peter 2:21-25

> **For even Christ pleased not himself; but, as it is written,**
> **The reproaches of them that reproached thee fell on me**
> **[Rom. 15:3].**

The quotation here is from Psalm 69:9. This is an imprecatory psalm and also one of the great messianic psalms. Christ never put His own interest and pleasures first. Stifler thinks that Christ is presented here as an argument rather than as an example. In *The Epistle to the Romans* (p. 250) he writes, "The Scriptures are not in the habit of holding up Christ as an example, for men are neither saved nor sanctified by an example." Always when Christ is given as an example it is in connection with the redeeming grace of God.

CONSOLIDATION OF JEWS AND GENTILES
IN ONE BODY

Paul now begins to talk about the fact that Jews and Gentiles are in one body to glorify God.

> **For whatsoever things were written aforetime were written for our learning, that we through patience and comfort of the scriptures might have hope [Rom. 15:4].**

The Old Testament, therefore, does have a definite application to believers today. I frequently receive letters from folk who say, "I didn't know the Old Testament was so practical," or, "I had not realized that the Old Testament had such meaning for us today. I did not know it spoke of Christ as it does. Paul here says that it was written for "our learning."

In my opinion, the greatest sin in the church of Jesus Christ in this generation is ignorance of the Word of God. Many times I have heard a church officer say, "Well, I don't know much about the Bible, but . . ." and then he gives his opinion, which often actually contradicts the Word of God! Why doesn't he know much about the Bible? These things were written aforetime for our learning. God wants you to *know* His Word. As an officer of the church, are you boasting that you are ignorant of the Word of God? Well, you had better get down to business and find out what God has said to you in His Word. Ignorance of the Bible is the greatest sin of the hour—in and out of the church. Paul says these things were written for your learning.

What will a knowledge of the Bible do for you? "That we through patience and comfort of the scriptures might have hope." The Word of God imparts patience, comfort, and hope.

You won't find any hope in the daily newspaper. You won't find any hope in modern literature. Look at any field and see if you can find any hope. There is none whatsoever. It is dark and dismal when you look out at this world today. My friend, the only place you can find real hope is in the Word of God.

I was in the state of Washington, speaking at a Bible conference, and it rained and rained and rained. Then it rained some more. Oh, how dark and dismal the days were! For our flight back home we went to the airport, and it was still raining. The plane took off and went up through a heavy layer of cloud. In a few moments we broke out into the light—the sun was shining up there. Oh, how beautiful it was. Less than a mile up, the sun was shining. Here we had been living like a bunch of gophers in all that rain. Now, don't misunderstand me— Washington needs all that rain to grow that lush vegetation and beautiful trees. But because I live in Southern California, I am used to sunshine, and I love it.

There are a great many Christians today who are living down beneath the clouds. The Lord says, "Come on up here and get in the sunshine of hope!" That is what the Bible will do for you, my friend. Paul wrote to the Corinthians: "Now all these things happened unto them for ensamples: and they are written for our admonition, upon whom the ends of the world are come" (1 Cor. 10:11). When I was teaching the life of David, scores of people told me what an encouragement David was to them. One person said that he was going through a very dark period in his life and that the study in the life of David delivered him from suicide. Well, that is the reason God put these things in His Word. God put David's sin on display—and it wasn't very nice—but God paints mankind exactly as he is for our *learning*. Everything in the Old Testament is written for our learning and to give us patience and to give us comfort and to bring hope into our lives.

Now the God of patience and consolation grant you to be likeminded one toward another according to Christ Jesus [Rom. 15:5].

Paul pauses here to pray that the blessings which are channeled only through the Word of God might have their effect upon both Jews and Gentiles in the body of Christ; not that they should see eye to eye with each other on meats and drink—they won't—but that they might demonstrate that they are one in love and consideration one of another.

**That ye may with one mind and one mouth glorify God,
even the Father of our Lord Jesus Christ [Rom. 15:6].**

There should be such a harmony in their praise that they reveal the unity of believers. When I was a boy in West Texas, we had a Methodist church on one corner, a Baptist church on another corner, and a Presbyterian church on the third corner. A story was told that one night the Methodists were singing, "Will there be any stars in my crown?" And the Presbyterians were singing, "No, not one; no, not one." And the Baptists were singing, "Oh, that will be glory for me." Well, that is just a story. I'm sure it never worked out that way, but sometimes it actually looks like that. However, if the Baptists and Methodists and Presbyterians are really believers (just to be a member of one of these denominations doesn't make you a believer, by the way), all three could sit down and sing the doxology together: "Praise God from whom all blessings flow." That is the testimony we should give to the world.

**Wherefore receive ye one another, as Christ also re-
ceived us to the glory of God [Rom. 15:7].**

Let me give you my translation of this: Wherefore receive ye one another, even as Christ also received you to the glory of God.

God receives man—both strong and weak, high and low, Jew and Gentile—on the simple acceptance of Christ. Now let both the strong and the weak receive each other in fellowship. The glory of God is the supreme objective.

A man said to me the other day, "Since you are very critical of the Pentecostal point of view, why is it that Pentecostal brethren are friendly toward you and actually invite you to speak in their churches?" I said, "Well, the reason is that they have more of the grace of God than I have." A recent letter from a Pentecostal pastor read, "We agree on too many things to let one or two differences separate us." When we agree on the major doctrines of the faith, though we may differ on minor points, we need to receive one another, as Christ also received us to the glory of God. Although I disagree with Pentecostal brethren on the matter of tongues, I see no reason why I should break fellowship with them. I just pray they will see it as I see it. And the very interesting thing is that one of these days, when we are in His presence, we will agree. In fact, all will agree with me. Do you know why? Because I am going to have to change a whole lot of things also. All of us will be changed, changed into His image and His likeness. Then all of us will agree. In view of that fact, we had better concentrate on the areas in which there is agreement now.

> Now I say that Jesus Christ was a minister of the circumcision for the truth of God, to confirm the promises made unto the fathers: *we were not made to the loses made slave*
>
> And that the Gentiles might glorify God for his mercy; as it is written, For this cause I will confess to thee among the Gentiles, and sing unto thy name [Rom. 15:8–9]. *Clean the heart not only the physical men*

When the Lord Jesus Christ came into this world, He came as "a minister of the circumcision"—this is the only time it is mentioned. His ministry was confined to the nation Israel. He frankly said so Himself: "But he answered and said, I am not sent but unto the lost sheep of the house of Israel" (Matt. 15:24). Also He directed His disciples: "But go rather to the lost sheep of the house of Israel" (Matt. 10:6). Christ came to earth about nineteen hundred years ago. He came in this capacity to confirm the promises made to Abraham, Isaac, and Jacob. God said that from the loins of Abraham He would bring One who would be a blessing to the world. Christ came to be a blessing to both Jew and Gentile. "And when eight days were accomplished for the circumcising of the child, his name was called JESUS, which was so named of the angel before he was conceived in the womb" (Luke 2:21). He could not have been "Jesus" unless He had been born in the line of Abraham and David and unless He followed the Law. They called Him Jesus after he was circumcised. He came to fulfill the entire Mosaic system. "But when the fulness of the time was come, God sent forth his Son, made of a woman, made under the law, to redeem them that were under the law, that we might receive the adoption of sons" (Gal. 4:4–5). Salvation came to Israel through Christ in confirming and fulfilling the truth of the Old Testament promises. Also by this method salvation was brought to the Gentiles. The Gentiles' only claim was upon the mercy of God. No promise was ever made to their fathers. I do not know who my father was, way back in the beginning in the forests of Germany and in Scotland. I do not know his name. But I do know that God never made any promise to him. He did, however, make a promise to Abraham, Isaac, and Jacob. Christ came to confirm the truth of the promises made to the fathers of the Jews, and He also came that the Gentiles might obtain mercy. In this the Gentiles are to glorify God. I thank God that He brought the gospel to my ancestors. They were pagan and savage and had done nothing to merit God's grace.

"As it is written" introduces four quotations from the Old Testament that show that the Gentiles are to praise God.

"For this cause I will confess to thee among the Gentiles, and sing unto thy name" is a quotation from Psalm 18:49. Christ is praising God through the Gentiles, which implies their conversion.

And again he saith, Rejoice, ye Gentiles, with his people [Rom. 15:10].

This quotation is from Deuteronomy 32:43. It concludes the song of Moses, which is a prophetic recitation of the history of the nation Israel until the coming of the millennial Kingdom. Here the Gentiles are invited to join Israel in praise to God.

And again, Praise the Lord, all ye Gentiles; and laud him, all ye people [Rom. 15:11].

This is a quotation from the briefest psalm (see Ps. 117:1). It is an invitation to the Gentiles to join Israel in praise to God. It is interesting to note the occurrence of the word *all* twice in this brief quotation.

And again, Esaias saith, There shall be a root of Jesse, and he that shall rise to reign over the Gentiles; in him shall the Gentiles trust [Rom. 15:12].

This quotation is from Isaiah 11:10. Though the Messiah is from the line of David, He is to rule over the Gentiles. Obviously it was the clear intention of God that the Gentiles should come to Christ. Some had come to Christ in Paul's day, and they were the firstfruits of even a greater day. Remember that Paul was writing to the Romans, and the Roman church was largely a gentile church, as are our churches today.

Now the God of hope fill you with all joy and peace in believing, that ye may abound in hope, through the power of the Holy Ghost [Rom. 15:13].

"The God of hope" is a new title for God which is thrilling. The believing heart finds here the Rock of Ages who is the shelter in the time of storm. "The God of hope fill you with all joy and peace in believing." This is what a study of Romans should do for you. I trust it has given you joy and peace and that it has strengthened your faith. I trust it has brought hope and power into your life, my friend.

This is the benediction that concludes the doctrinal section of the Epistle to the Romans.

CONTINUATION OF PAUL'S PERSONAL TESTIMONY

At this point Paul resumes his personal testimony as an apostle to the Gentiles. You remember that he began this epistle in a very personal manner. Now he leaves the doctrinal section, and he picks up that personal note with which he began the epistle, in which he expressed the desire to visit Rome. "Now at length I might have a prosperous journey by the will of God to come unto you" (Rom. 1:10). Now listen to him.

> **And I myself also am persuaded of you, my brethren, that ye also are full of goodness, filled with all knowledge, able also to admonish one another [Rom. 15:14].**

This, I think, is one of the loveliest passages. Paul is offering in this verse a gentle apology for his frankness and boldness in speaking to the Romans in the doctrinal section. It was not because they were lacking in goodness and knowledge, but rather because they possessed these qualities that Paul was able to be so explicit. Isn't that wonderful? He gave us the Epistle to the Romans so that he could talk to us about these important issues. My friend, an understanding of the Epistle to the Romans is an essential part of your Christian growth. Every Christian should make an effort to know Romans, for this book will ground the believer in the faith. Paul is being very humble and sweet about his exhortations in this epistle. He is not lording it over God's heritage.

> **Nevertheless, brethren, I have written the more boldly unto you in some sort, as putting you in mind, because of the grace that is given to me of God,**

> **That I should be the minister of Jesus Christ to the Gentiles, ministering the gospel of God, that the offering up of the Gentiles might be acceptable, being sanctified by the Holy Ghost [Rom. 15:15–16].**

When Paul says, "I have written," he is referring to this Epistle to the Romans. He is explaining the fact of his boldness by reminding the Romans that he is the apostle to the Gentiles. On the basis of this God-appointed office, which came to him through the grace of God, he is exercising that office in writing as he does to the Romans. He is ministering to them. This statement gives added weight to the inspiration of the writings of Paul. He adopts the language of the Levitical temple worship in describing himself as a minister preaching the gospel.

The Gentiles are "acceptable"—apart from the Law or any religion—through Christ as preached by Paul.

"Sanctified"—the Holy Spirit indwelt the gentile believers, beginning with Cornelius. The sanctifying work of the Holy Spirit begins with Jew and Gentile the *moment* of regeneration when the Spirit of God takes up His abode within the believer. Paul gave the gospel, but God gave the Holy Spirit when they believed. It must be kept in mind that Paul was the apostle to the Gentiles in a very special sense. As a high priest, Paul offered up the Gentiles, making an offering unto God. It is difficult for us today to fathom the full significance of all this, and yet we as Gentiles have entered into all that this implies. My friend, if you have never thanked God for the apostle Paul, you should thank Him right now. God gave Paul to us. For this reason we should read his Epistle to the Romans.

> **I have therefore whereof I may glory through Jesus Christ in those things which pertain to God [Rom. 15:17].**

Paul had written boldly to the Romans and was rather apologetic about it because he recognized that these saints in Rome probably did not need his instructions. In spite of this, however, he wrote with confidence to them. There is no personal assumption in this, He is a servant of Christ Jesus and is doing His will. This is important to see. There is one thing that should never characterize a servant of God, and that is pride. We should never become officious, but rather take the position that we are merely serving the Lord Jesus Christ, and He is the One in charge.

> **For I will not dare to speak of any of those things which Christ hath not wrought by me, to make the Gentiles obedient, by word and deed,**
>
> **Through mighty signs and wonders, by the power of the Spirit of God; so that from Jerusalem, and round about unto Illyricum, I have fully preached the gospel of Christ [Rom. 15:18–19].**

Paul is saying something very important in this passage. If we are to understand Paul, and especially whether he or Peter founded the church at Rome, we must pay close attention to what he says here. Paul is saying, "I will not take credit for the work of God that is being done by others—especially among the Gentiles." Of course he couldn't take credit for what was accomplished on the Day of Pentecost, which was the beginning of the ministry that resulted in the gospel going to the Gentiles. He couldn't take credit for the gospel going to the first Gentiles. It was Simon Peter who took the gospel to the home of Cornelius. Paul will speak only of those things which Christ wrought by him. He had a peculiar ministry as the apostle to the Gentiles.

"Through mighty signs and wonders," which were the credentials of the apostles and the ministers in the early church. These were given to establish the church on the right foundation before a word of the New Testament had been written. Paul, speaking to the Ephesian believers, says that they ". . . are built upon the foundation of the apostles and prophets, Jesus Christ himself being the chief corner stone" (Eph. 2:20). He does not intend to say that the apostles are the foundation. There is no foundation but Christ: "For other foundation can no man lay than that is laid, which is Jesus Christ" (1 Cor. 3:11). But the apostles are the ones who put down the foundation of Jesus Christ. That is what Paul is saying here.

Paul says that the gospel of Christ had come through him "unto Illyricum." Illyricum was a province of the Roman Empire next to Italy. It extended to the Adriatic Sea and the Danube River. Paul, you see, had preached by this time from Jerusalem to the province next to Rome. He had not quite reached Rome. By the way, we have no record of Paul's journey in this area. Undoubtedly he went many places that are not detailed for us. There are those who believe that Paul went to Spain. I believe this epistle reveals that he did go to Spain, and I think he also went to Great Britain because he covered the Roman Empire, as we shall see.

Yea, so have I strived to preach the gospel, not where Christ was named, lest I should build upon another man's foundation:

But as it is written, To whom he was not spoken of, they shall see: and they that have not heard shall understand [Rom. 15:20-21].

Perhaps my translation will make these verses a little clearer: Indeed, in this way having made it my ambition to preach the gospel, not where Christ was named, in order that I might not be building upon another man's foundation: but as it is written, They shall see, those to whom there came no tidings of Him, and those who have not heard shall understand.

It was a point of honor with Paul—not competition—which caused him to go as a pioneer where the gospel had not been preached. Paul had a peculiar ministry. Paul did not minister where a church already existed or where others had gone. He was a true missionary, which is the meaning of the word *evangelist* in the New Testament. Paul never had a committee to do the groundwork ahead of him. When Paul entered a town, he was not given a welcome. The mayor did not greet him. If anyone greeted him, it was usually the chief of police, who generally arrested him and put him in jail. Since the apostles laid the foundation, the believers would have to be very careful to discern who the apostles were and to whom they were listening. Paul had the credentials God had given to the apostles. It is said of Paul and Barnabus, "Long time therefore abode they speaking boldly in the Lord, which gave testimony unto the word of his grace, and granted signs and wonders to be done by their hands" (Acts 14:3). You see, these were the marks of the apostles and the early preachers of the gospel. They did not come with a New Testament in their hands—it hadn't been written yet. They came with these credentials: mighty "signs and wonders."

Of course the day came when signs and wonders were no longer the identifying mark. The apostle John, near the end of his long life, wrote: "If there come any unto you, and bring not this doctrine, receive him not into your house, neither bid him God speed" (2 John 10). Correct doctrine was the identifying mark for a man of God even then. And today the identifying mark is correct doctrine, not signs and wonders.

A tragic movement is going on at this writing. Coming to my desk is literally a flood of letters from people who are being carried away by fantacism, by wrong teaching, and by false doctrine. Although there is a movement of the Holy Spirit today, there is also a movement of the Devil. Satan is busy. A great many people are being carried away and trapped by incorrect teaching. Paul has been so careful to emphasize the fact that the kingdom of God is not meat and drink. Well, the kingdom of God is not signs and wonders either. It is not any of these outward things. The Kingdom of God just happens to be righteousness. I hear of groups meeting and indulging in all kinds of sexual rites—not living for God at all—yet talking about certain signs that they demonstrate, such as speaking in tongues. My friend, it had better be a *clean* tongue. If the Lord has come into your life, He will clean you up. A clean tongue and one that declares the Word of God accurately is what a great many folk need today. Paul always ministered where the gospel had not previously gone. He was a true evangelist, a true missionary.

Since Paul said that he did not go where the gospel had been preached before, who is the founder of the church in Rome? He makes it very clear, both in his introduction and at this point, that he is the founder of the church in Rome.

In Romans 16 we will be introduced to a group of people in Rome whom Paul knew. The record tells us that Paul led them to the Lord. He reached these people out in the Roman Empire and many of them gravitated to Rome. There they met together around the person of the Lord Jesus. I am sure they talked many times about their beloved pastor, Paul. He founded the church, not by going there in person, but by remote control—you might say, by spiritual radar.

"To whom he was not spoken of, they shall see: and they that have not heard shall understand" seems to be Paul's life verse as a missionary. It is a quotation of Isaiah 52:15 from the Septuagint version. Paul was thrilled to go and preach the gospel to those who were spiritually blind. After Paul had preached, some brother would say, "I understand, brother Paul. I will accept Christ as my Savior." My friend, there is no thrill equal to presenting Christ and having people turn to Him.

For which cause also I have been much hindered from coming to you [Rom. 15:22].

When Paul says that he had been "much hindered," you may be sure of one thing: he was *much* hindered. Many roadblocks had been put in his way.

But now having no more place in these parts, and having a great desire these many years to come unto you;

Whensoever I take my journey into Spain, I will come to you: for I trust to see you in my journey, and to be brought on my way thitherward by you, if first I be somewhat filled with your company [Rom. 15:23–24].

Paul makes it clear that he wants to take the gospel way out yonder and that he is coming to Rome. Now he says something unusually strange: "But now having no more place in these parts." There is a question about what Paul meant by this. Was he saying that there was no longer an opportunity to preach the gospel in the section of the Roman Empire where he was at that time? Had the doors completely closed to him? Had everyone been saved? Had every nook and cranny been evangelized? I used to take the position that the answer was "no" to these questions. However, now that I have visited the sites of the seven churches of Asia Minor, I'm not sure that I was right, because Paul and the other witnesses had been faithful, and the gospel had been sounded out through the entire area. The Word had gone out. Dr. Luke says that everyone, both Jew and Gentile, had heard the gospel. This does not mean that they all had turned to Christ, but they all had heard. Now Paul is looking for new territory. He has his eyes on the frontier of the empire. He says, "Whensoever I take my journey into Spain, I will come to you." In other words, Rome was not his destination. He wanted to go to Spain. He had come from one end of the Roman Empire, and he wanted to go to the other end of the Roman Empire. He says, "For I trust to see you in my journey, and to be brought on my way witherward by you." You see, Rome was not his terminal. He wanted to go all the way to the other end of the empire.

The question is: Did Paul ever go to Spain? If he did, we have no record of it. But neither have we a record of his journey to Illyricum; we would not know he had been there if he had not mentioned it in verse 19. Personally I believe that Paul did go to Spain and to the rest of the Roman Empire. My reason is a statement that he made when he came to the end of his life. He said, "I have fought a good fight, I have finished my course, I have kept the faith" (2 Tim. 4:7). Paul said he had finished his course. I don't think he would have said that if he had not been to Spain, because Spain was on his itinerary.

Paul wanted to go to Spain and he also wanted to go to Jerusalem.

But now I go unto Jerusalem to minister unto the saints.

For it hath pleased them of Macedonia and Achaia to make a certain contribution for the poor saints which are at Jerusalem [Rom. 15:25–26].

He wanted to go to Jerusalem to take a gift to the poor saints there, and he wanted to take it with his own hands. Why? Because with his own hands he had "wasted" the church at Jerusalem; he had led in the persecution of the believers in Jerusalem. Now it was in the heart of this great apostle to make up for that by taking a gift to them.

"A certain contribution." The Greek word which is translated "contribution" is koinōnia, meaning "a fellowship." This word was used for everything that believers could share: Christ, the Word, prayer, the Lord's Supper, and material gifts. Christians have fellowship with God, with Christ, and with one another when they give. Fellowship is not just patting somebody on the back. The knife and fork clubs meet every week, and that is fellowship as far as they are concerned. But for a believer, fellowship is sharing the things of Christ. Paul is talking here about going to Jerusalem where previously he had persecuted the church. Now he wants to have fellowship with them; he wants to take a gift to them. In Acts we have the historical record of this: Paul said, "Now after many years I came to bring alms to my nation, and offerings" (Acts 24:17). This collection was very important to Paul. We find him writing about it in 2 Corinthians—in fact, chapters 8 and 9 deal with it.

> **It hath pleased them verily; and their debtors they are.**
> **For if the Gentiles have been made partakers of their**
> **spiritual things, their duty is also to minister unto them**
> **in carnal things [Rom. 15:27].**

Paul makes it clear that it was a freewill offering. "Every man according as he purposeth in his heart, so let him give; not grudgingly, or of necessity: for God loveth a cheerful giver" (2 Cor. 9:7). This is the offering Paul collected. Paul makes it very clear that it not only was a freewill offering (they couldn't give any other way to please God), but he also enforces the fact that they had a moral obligation and debt to pay. The Gentiles had received the gospel from Israel. Our Lord Jesus said, "Ye worship ye know not what: we know what we worship: for salvation is of the Jews" (John 4:22). You see, the gospel began in Jerusalem. Macedonia and Achaia were *obligated* to Jerusalem. Now some of the saints in Jerusalem were having financial difficulties, evidently because of persecution. Macedonia and Achaia could now pay a spiritual debt in the coin of the realm. This is foreign missions in reverse! It is the missionary church helping the home church. This very thing may take place in our nation, by the way, in the not too far distant future!

> **When therefore I have performed this, and have sealed**
> **to them this fruit, I will come by you into Spain [Rom.**
> **15:28].**

You can see that this gift was on the heart of the great apostle Paul—notice the zeal he had in taking it to Jerusalem. That trip, of course, placed him into the hands of his enemies who had him arrested. I disagree with some of my brethren who believe that Paul was out of the will of God during this time. I maintain that Paul was absolutely in the will of God when he went up to Jerusalem, as we have seen in the Book of Acts.

"And have sealed to them this fruit" is an awkward phrase for us and could mean no more than that he wanted a receipt for the offering. He secured to them the gift. It probably means that he wanted the Jerusalem church to see some fruits of their missionary efforts. I personally believe that if you are going to contribute money to some cause, you ought to know what it is doing. The area of Christian giving is one of grave danger today. I do not believe, Christian friend, that you should give to any work unless you know two things about it: (1) what it is doing, and (2) is it getting out the Word of God in a way that is effectual in hearts and lives?

And I am sure that, when I come unto you, I shall come in the fulness of the blessing of the gospel of Christ [Rom. 15:29].

This is Paul's stamp of approval on his prosperous journey to Rome. He went there according to the will of God and in the fullness of his apostolic office. God gave him divine insight into this trip. Paul is not out of the will of God in going to Jerusalem. Neither was he out of the will of God in going to Rome. It may not look like a prosperous journey, but God used it that way. It is very easy for God's children, when trouble comes and things look dark and doubtful, to say, "I must be out of the will of God." My friend, just because you have trouble and disturbed feelings does not mean that you are of God's will. In fact, it may definitely mean you are in His will. If you are living in perfect calm today and nothing is happening, the chances are you are not in His will.

Now I beseech you, brethren, for the Lord Jesus Christ's sake, and for the love of the Spirit, that ye strive together with me in your prayers to God for me [Rom. 15:30].

I have been dwelling a long time in this area. One reason is that this is a personal area, and Paul is laying bare his heart. The second reason is that we are seeing how Christianity functioned in the first century. We are seeing the practical side of Christianity. In the first part of Romans Paul gave us doctrine. Now Paul is putting that doctrine into practice.

This is one of the most solemn, earnest, and serious appeals of Paul for prayer that we find in the Bible. He says, "I beg of you, brethren, through our Lord Jesus Christ, and through the love of the Spirit, that ye strive intensely with me in your prayers to God on behalf of me." Paul recognizes that he is facing danger and has come to a crisis in his ministry. Enemies are on every hand. Paul had reason to fear, as succeeding events proved. He is asking for prayer in a very wonderful way, "through our Lord Jesus Christ." Paul realized that everything that was to come to him had to come through Jesus Christ. He asked the believers in Rome to join with him in prayer. He says, "I want all of you to pray through Christ—He is our great Intercessor—go through Him to God on my behalf."

By "through the love of the Spirit" he means that love is the fruit of the Spirit which joins all believers together. And, friend, we ought to pray for each other.

"That ye strive intensely for me." The Greek word for *strive* is tremendous. We get our English word *agonize* from it. Paul is saying, "Agonize with me."

"On behalf of me"—he is asking for prayer for his personal safety that he might come in "the fulness of the blessing of the gospel of Christ." Oh, my friend, how we need to pray like this—not just praying by rote or by going over our prayer list hurriedly. For the apostle Paul prayer was with great agony, great exercise of soul. He laid hold of God. This kind of praying is so desperately needed today! You and I need people who know how to pray for us.

That I may be delivered from them that do not believe in Judaea; and that my service which I have for Jerusalem may be accepted of the saints [Rom. 15:31].

In other words, this is Paul's prayer request, and it is twofold. His life was in jeopardy from unbelievers in Judea, the religious rulers. He wanted to be delivered from them. Secondly, the church in Jerusalem might be hesitant in accepting a gift from Gentiles, and he wanted them to accept it. My friend, both requests were answered. Somebody says, "Yes, but he was arrested." Right, but he was immediately put into the hands of the Romans and was enabled to appear before kings, and finally he actually appeared before the Caesar in Rome, which was the fulfillment of the will of God for the apostle Paul.

That I may come unto you with joy by the will of God, and may with you be refreshed [Rom. 15:32].

This is the conclusion of Paul's prayer request. The prayer was answered: his life was spared, the church in Jerusalem accepted the gift, he did come with joy to Rome—in spite of the fact that he spent two years in jail at Caesarea, was shipwrecked on the way, and when he arrived in Rome he was in chains. Yet Paul came in the joy of the Holy Spirit. Oh, how all of us need that kind of joy in our lives!

Did Paul find rest and refreshment in Rome? Well, the answer is debatable. He did find all this and more beyond Rome and Spain when he entered the presence of Christ. He wrote near the end of his life to Timothy, his son in the faith: "For I am now ready to be offered, and the time of my departure is at hand. I have fought a good fight, I have finished my course, I have kept the faith: Henceforth there is laid up for me a crown of righteousness, which the Lord, the righteous judge, shall give me at that day: and not to me only, but unto all them also that love his appearing" (2 Tim. 4:6–8).

This chapter concludes with Paul's benediction:

Now the God of peace be with you all. Amen [Rom. 15:33].

"The God of peace" shows that Paul experienced peace in prison, in chains, in storm, and in shipwreck. I pray that you and I might have that kind of peace in our lives.

CHAPTER 16

THEME: Commendation of Phebe; Christians in Rome greeted; conduct toward other Christians; Christians with Paul send greetings; benediction

In this final chapter of Romans the gospel walks in shoe leather in the first century of the Roman Empire. It thrills my heart to know that in the pagan Roman Empire there were Christians, witnesses for Christ, walking down the streets of those cities with the joy of the Lord in their hearts. I consider this one of the most revealing chapters that we have in the Epistle to the Romans. Paul has left the mountain peaks of doctrine to come down to the pavements of Rome. Here we see Christianity in action. The great doctrines which Paul proclaimed are not missiles for outer space. They are vehicles which actually operated on Roman roads. The gospel was translated into life and reality. This remarkable chapter should not be omitted or neglected in any study of Romans. William R. Newell has well said, "The sixteenth chapter is neglected by many to their own loss" (*Romans Verse by Verse*, p. 548).

There are thirty-five persons mentioned by name in this chapter. All were either believers living in Rome or they were believers who were with the apostle Paul—he was probably in Corinth when he wrote this epistle. There is expressed a mutual love and tender affection which was a contradiction of Roman philosophy and practice. (Also, it is rather unlike some churches today!) These Christians were different. Little wonder that Rome marveled at these folk and exclaimed, "My, how these Christians love each other!"

COMMENDATION OF PHEBE

The chapter begins with a commendation of Phebe, the woman who brought this epistle to Rome.

I command unto Phebe our sister, which is a servant of
the church which is at Cenchrea:

That ye receive her in the Lord, as becometh saints, and
that ye assist her in whatsoever business she hath need
of you: for she hath been a succourer of many, and of
myself also [Rom. 16:1–2].

Phebe is the first believer mentioned in this, another catalog of the
heroes of the faith. She was a Gentile, as her name indicates. As I have
already stated, there were many Gentiles in the church at Rome. She
was named for the Greek goddess, Artemis or Diana, who in Greek
mythology was the goddess of the moon, as her brother, Apollo, was
the god of the sun. Many believers adopted new names at baptism, but
Phebe kept her heathen name for some reason.

Phebe was the bearer of the Epistle to the Romans. Apparently she
was a very prominent woman in the church, which means she was a
woman of ability. She is called a "servant of the church which is at
Cenchrea." Cenchrea is the eastern seaport of Corinth. When I stood at
the ruins of ancient Corinth, I looked down and saw in the distance
Cenchrea. On that clear day, it looked much closer than the eight or
nine miles it is said to be. Apparently Paul wrote the Epistle to the
Romans while he was at Corinth, and Phebe, who may have been a
woman of means or engaged in business, took it with her to Rome. She
is called a servant of the church, which means she was a deaconess.
The Greek word *diakonos* is the same word used for deacon. It reveals
the fact that women occupied a very prominent place in the early
church.

It is my feeling that we would not be seeing women today occupy-
ing the position of pastors in the church (which is forbidden by Scripture) if they had been given their rightful position in the church. I
think they should be deaconesses in the church and that they should
sit on an equality with any other board of the church. The church
needs some of the insights and sensibilities that women possess. God
has made a woman finer than a man, just as a watch is finer than an
automobile. She has been given a sense that man doesn't have. For

instance, she can watch a woman who is a complete stranger to her, and in five minutes she knows a great deal about her simply by observing her dress and her manner. Those of us who belong to the male side of the human race appear stupid at a time like that. We can see if she is good looking or not, but that is the extent of our observation. The church needs the insight that a woman has.

Paul apparently put into Phebe's hand this Epistle to the Romans rather than trusting it to public transportation. Rome did have mail service, but it was slow. Paul, you see, is going back to Jerusalem, and Phebe brings his epistle with her to Rome.

"I commend unto you Phebe our sister"—Paul commends her to the believers there at Rome. She is the first woman mentioned in this final chapter.

CHRISTIANS IN ROME GREETED

Now Paul sends his greetings to quite a list of Christian folk.

Greet Priscilla and Aquila my helpers in Christ Jesus:

Who have for my life laid down their own necks: unto whom not only I give thanks, but also all the churches of the Gentiles [Rom. 16:3–4].

At this time there were gentile churches, you see, and I believe the church at Rome was largely gentile, made up of many races. It was integrated for sure.

"Priscilla and Aquila" were a Jewish couple. How had Paul met them, and in what way were they his helpers? Well, there had been a wave of anti-Semitism that had swept over the city of Rome, and Priscilla and Aquila had had to leave. They came to the city of Corinth while Paul was there and set up shop. Corinth was a good commercial center, and Paul was also plying his trade there. Since they were all tentmakers, this drew them together (see Acts 18:1–3), and Paul led them to the Lord. Then they were with Paul at Ephesus. Perhaps they had gone over there to open up a branch store. In Acts 18:26, we find that they were able to be helpful to Apollos: "And he [Apollos] began to speak boldly in the synagogue: whom when Aquila and Priscilla had heard, they took him unto them, and expounded unto him the way of God more perfectly." Notice that when we first meet them it is "Aquila and Priscilla." Now here in Romans it is Priscilla and Aquila. Why are the names reversed? Well, I think here is a case when the woman became dominant in spiritual matters. Spiritually she became the leader, although they were both outstanding workers for Christ.

> **Likewise greet the church that is in their house. Salute my well-beloved Epaenetus, who is the firstfruits of Achaia unto Christ [Rom. 16:5].**

The local church met in private homes at the very beginning. (See Acts 12:12; 1 Cor. 16:19; Col. 4:15; Philem. 2.) Sanday writes, "There is no decisive evidence until the third century of the existence of special buildings used for churches." It is the belief of many folk today, and I have found this belief for years, that the church which began in the home will return to meeting in the home. Many of these great big buildings we call churches, with great steeples on them, are nothing more than a pile of brick, stone, and mortar. They are mausoleums, not living churches that contain a real, living body of believers. The church was never intended to be spoken of as a building. For the first three centuries the church was the body of believers and met in homes like that of Aquila and Priscilla.

Epaenetus is a Greek name meaning "praised." Evidently he was Paul's first convert in the Roman province of Achaia.

> **Greet Mary, who bestowed much labour on us [Rom. 16:6].**

Mary is a Jewish name, the same as Miriam, meaning "rebelliousness." She "bestowed much labour on us" means that she labored to the point of exhaustion. What a change had taken place in her life! Before becoming a believer, she was in rebellion, but now she "knocks herself out" for the sake of other believers, because she is now obedient to Christ.

> Salute Andronicus and Junia, my kinsmen, and my fellowprisoners, who are of note among the apostles, who also were in Christ before me [Rom. 16:7].

Andronicus is a Greek name, and the name has been identified with a slave.

Junia is a Roman name and can be either masculine or feminine. Paul calls them "my fellow countrymen," which may mean that they belonged to the tribe of Benjamin as did Paul. It does not necessarily mean close blood relationship.

Paul says, they were "my fellow prisoners." Evidently Paul had met them in one of the numerous prisons of the Roman Empire. These two were well–known to the apostles and were held in high regard by them. Paul had not led them to Christ, as is the natural assumption, for they were in Christ before he was.

The church in Rome was founded by Paul under most unusual circumstances. He had met Aquila and Priscilla in the Corinthian agora, the marketplace, and then he met these two men in jail. These had then gone to Rome and formed the church there.

> Greet Amplias my beloved in the Lord.

> Salute Urbane, our helper in Christ, and Stachys my beloved [Rom. 16:8–9].

Amplias is a common slave name and occurs in the tombs of the early Christians in the catacombs, always in a place of honor. He evidently was one of Paul's converts and dear to his heart.

Urbane means "city bred." In other words, his name actually means "city-slicker." This was also a common slave name, and it may mean that he was brought up in the city rather than in the country. He is identified as a real worker among believers.

Stachys has been found listed in the royal household. It is a masculine name. He was beloved not only to Paul but to the church.

> **Salute Apelles approved in Christ. Salute them which are of Aristobulus' household [Rom. 16:10].**

Apelles is the approved one. His is either a Greek or a Jewish name—the name was a common one among the Jews. He had stood some outstanding test. Tradition identifies him as bishop either of Smyrna or Heracleia.

Aristobulus has been identified by Bishop Lightfoot as the grandson of Herod the Great. Or possibly he was a slave who took the name of his master—we can't be sure of this.

> **Salute Herodian my kinsman. Greet them that be of the household of Narcissus, which are in the Lord [Rom. 16:11].**

Herodian was evidently a Jew, as Paul calls him a fellow countryman. The name suggests the Herod family. He may have been a slave who adopted the name of the family to which he belonged.

Narcissus is the name of a well-known freedman put to death by Agrippina. The one whose name appears here was probably a slave who formerly belonged to him and had taken his name.

> **Salute Tryphena and Tryphosa, who labour in the Lord. Salute the beloved Persis, which laboured much in the Lord [Rom. 16:12].**

Tryphena and *Tryphosa* are euphonious names that mean "delicate" and "dainty." I imagine these two little ladies were old maid sisters who came to know Christ. They may have been women of means, and they had supported the apostle Paul. Paul says that they labored "in the Lord"—they were real workers in the church at Rome.

"The beloved Persis" is another woman who "laboured *much* in the Lord." *Persis* is the name of a freedwoman, and her position may have enabled her to do more than the preceding two sisters.

Salute Rufus chosen in the Lord, and his mother and mine [Rom. 16:13].

Although this man seems to stand in the shadows in this chapter, actually we can know a great deal about him—even to the color of his hair! His name means "red." *Red* was the name by which he was called. However, there were many red-haired folk; it was not his hair that made him unusual. The thing that marks him out is the phrase that follows, "chosen in the Lord." I love that. "But," you may say, "were not the others in this chapter chosen in the Lord also?" Yes, they were all wonderful saints, but this man was outstanding. Perhaps a better translation would be "distinguished in the Lord." He was a great saint of God.

That Rufus was prominent in the church is inferred in the reference to his father. When John Mark wrote his Gospel, he wrote it primarily for the Romans. In it he mentions the incident of a man by the name of Simon carrying the cross of Christ. "And they compel one Simon a Cyrenian, who passed by, coming out of the country, the father of Alexander and Rufus, to bear his cross" (Mark 15:21). The Roman soldiers that day saw Jesus falling under the cross. Looking over the crowd they shouted, "Here!" to a big double-fisted fellow, Simon of Cyrene. "You come here and carry it." And carry it he did—an act that has made him immortal. John Mark, writing to Rome, identifies Simon for them by adding, "the father of Alexander and Rufus"—all the saints at Rome would know Rufus because he was outstanding in the church.

Will you notice further that Paul's greeting includes the mother of Rufus. "Salute Rufus . . . and his mother and mine." While we know nothing of the mother of Paul the apostle and nothing of his father, we learn here of a godly woman in the city of Jerusalem, the wife of Simon the Cyrenian, who was like a mother to the apostle Paul. You may recall that the first time Paul came to Jerusalem following his conversion, the Christians feared him. They were unconvinced that this powerful Pharisee was genuine; they suspected trickery. Yet the mother of Rufus took Paul in, "You just come in and stay with Rufus in his room." Looking back to that time, Paul writes concerning her, "She is Rufus' mother, but she is mine also." What a lovely tribute to this warmhearted Christian mother!

> Salute Asyncritus, Phlegon, Hermas, Patrobas, Hermes, and the brethren which are with them [Rom. 16:14].

These are all just names to us, but Paul knew them. Probably he had led them to Christ.

> Salute Philologus, and Julia, Nereus, and his sister, and Olympas, and all the saints which are with them [Rom. 16:15].

Here is another group of believers who were in the church there in Rome.

CONDUCT TOWARD OTHER CHRISTIANS

> Salute one another with an holy kiss. The churches of Christ salute you [Rom. 16:16].

This was the formal greeting in Paul's time—I don't recommend it for today!

> Now I beseech you, brethren, mark them which cause divisions and offences contrary to the doctrine which ye have learned; and avoid them.

> For they that are such serve not our Lord Jesus Christ, but their own belly; and by good words and fair speeches deceive the hearts of the simple [Rom. 16:17–18].

Paul puts in this word of warning. We would do well to heed this warning also, my beloved.

> **For your obedience is come abroad unto all men. I am glad therefore on your behalf: but yet I would have you wise unto that which is good, and simple discerning evil [Rom. 16:19].**

You see, their faith came abroad also, but the faith is manifested in obedience.

"Wise unto that which is good" means they must be instructed in the Word of God.

"Simple concerning evil" means without a mixture of evil. To the Corinthians Paul said, "Brethren, be not children in understanding: howbeit in malice be ye children, but in understanding be men" (1 Cor. 14:20).

> **And the God of peace shall bruise Satan under your feet shortly. The grace of our Lord Jesus Christ be with you. Amen [Rom. 16:20].**

It is "the god of peace" who will put down Satan shortly. In the meantime we are to resist the Devil, be sober and vigilant.

CHRISTIANS WITH PAUL SEND GREETINGS

Now Paul sends greetings from those who were with him as he was writing this Epistle to the Romans.

> **Timotheus my workfellow, and Lucius, and Jason, and Sosipater, my kinsmen, salute you [Rom. 16:21].**

All of these were companions of Paul. They send greetings to their fellow believers in Rome.

> **I Tertius, who wrote this epistle, salute you in the Lord [Rom. 16:22].**

Paul, you see, had an amanuensis, a secretary, to write his letters. (The Epistle to the Galatians is the exception.)

> **Gaius mine host, and of the whole church, saluteth you. Erastus the chamberlain of the city saluteth you, and Quartus a brother [Rom. 16:23].**

Paul was staying in the home of Gaius, and Gaius wanted to send his salutations also.

> **The grace of our Lord Jesus Christ be with you all. Amen [Rom. 16:24].**

BENEDICTION

> **Now to him that is of power to stablish you according to my gospel, and the preaching of Jesus Christ, according to the revelation of the mystery, which was kept secret since the world began [Rom. 16:25].**

"The mystery" means that it had not been revealed in the Old Testament. It refers to the present age when God is taking both Jew and Gentile and fashioning them into one body, the church.

> **But now is made manifest, and by the scriptures of the prophets, according to the commandment of the everlasting God, made known to all nations for the obedience of faith [Rom. 16:26].**

Here we see the obedience of faith. When you trust Christ, you will obey Him, my friend. The Lord Jesus said, "My sheep hear my voice, and I know them, and they follow me" (John 10:27). Obedience is the work and fruit of faith.

My favorite hymn is "Trust and Obey" by John H. Sammis:

When we walk with the Lord
In the Light of His Word,
What a glory He sheds on our way!
While we do His good will,
He abides with us still,
And with all who will trust and obey.

Then in fellowship sweet
We will sit at His feet,
Or we'll walk by His side in the way;
What He says we will do,
Where He sends we will go—
Never fear, only trust and obey.

Trust and obey, for there's no other way
To be happy in Jesus, but to trust and obey.

To God only wise, be glory through Jesus Christ for ever. Amen [Rom. 16:27].

BIBLIOGRAPHY

(Recommended for Further Study)

Barnhouse, Donald Grey. *Romans*. 4 vols. Grand Rapids, Michigan: Wm. B. Eerdmans Publishing Co., 1952–1960. (Expositions of Bible doctrines, taking the Epistle to the Romans as a point of departure.)

DeHaan, Richard W. *The World on Trial: Studies in Romans*. Grand Rapids, Michigan: Zondervan Publishing House, 1970.

Epp, Theodore H. *How God Makes Bad Men Good: Studies in Romans*. Lincoln, Nebraska: Back to the Bible Broadcast, 1978.

Hendriksen, William. *The Epistle to the Romans*. Grand Rapids, Michigan: Baker Book House, 1980.

Hodge, Charles. *Commentary on the Epistle to the Romans*. Grand Rapids, Michigan: Wm. B. Eerdmans Publishing Co., 1886.

Hoyt, Herman A. *The First Christian Theology: Studies in Romans*. Grand Rapids, Michigan: Baker Book House, 1977. (Good for group study.)

Ironside, H. A. *Lectures on Romans*. Neptune, New Jersey: Loizeaux Brothers, n.d. (Especially fine for young Christians.)

Jensen, Irving R. *Romans: Self-Study Guide*. Chicago, Illinois: Moody Press, n.d.

Johnson, Alan F. *Romans: The Freedom Letter*. Chicago, Illinois: Moody Press, 1974.

Kelly, William. *Notes on Romans*. Addison, Illinois: Bible Truth Publishers, 1873.

Luther, Martin. *Commentary on Romans*. 1516 Reprint. Grand Rapids, Michigan: Kregel Publications, 1976.

McClain, Alva J. *Romans: The Gospel of God's Grace.* Chicago, Illinois: Moody Press, 1942.

McGee, J. Vernon. *Reasoning Through Romans.* 2 vols. Pasadena, California: Thru the Bible Books, 1959.

Moule, Handley C. G. *The Epistle to the Romans.* Fort Washington, Pennsylvania: Christian Literature Crusade, n.d. (See note below.)

Moule, Handley C. G. *Studies in Romans.* Grand Rapids, Michigan: Kregel Publications, 1892. (Originally appeared in the Cambridge Bible for Schools and Colleges. These two books by Moule complement each other and are both excellent.)

Murray, John. *Romans.* Grand Rapids, Michigan: Wm. B. Eerdmans Publishing Co., 1965. (For advanced students.)

Newell, William R. *Romans Verse by Verse.* Chicago, Illinois: Moody Press, 1938. (An excellent study.)

Philips, John. *Exploring Romans.* Chicago, Illinois: Moody Press, 1969.

Stifler, James. *The Epistle to the Romans.* Chicago, Illinois: Moody Press, 1897.

Thomas, W. H. Griffith. *The Book of Romans.* Grand Rapids, Michigan: Wm. B. Eerdmans Publishing Co., 1946. (Fine interpretation.)

Vine, W. E. *Romans.* Grand Rapids, Michigan: Zondervan Publishing House, 1950.

Wuest, Kenneth S. *Romans in the Greek New Testament for English Readers.* Grand Rapids, Michigan: Wm. B. Eerdmans Publishing Co., 1955.

Wiersbe, Warren W. *Be Right. (Romans).* Wheaton, Illinois: Victor Books, 1977.

1. Hope
2. Joy
3. Peace
4. Power

How do we see these in the body of Emmanuel Baptist Church? Where are we lacking?

The fruits of the spirit is Love, Joy, peace Patience, kindness, goodness, faithfulness Gentleness and self-control.